Praise for *How to Break Up with Your Friends*

"Don't let the title fool you—this is a book about connection, empathy, and finding nourishment through friendship. *How to Break Up with Your Friends* is an essential guide to creating space for these important relationships in our busy lives."

XIMENA VENGOECHEA
author of *Listen Like You Mean It*

"If you've ever been in a situation where ending a friendship felt as painful as a divorce, read this book now. *How to Break Up with Your Friends* is a manifesto for genuine friendship. Erin sheds light on the qualities of forming deeper connections, prioritizing our well-being, and setting boundaries within our existing relationships, and, ultimately, how to have the courageous conversations needed when it's time to 'break up.'"

JUSTIN MICHAEL WILLIAMS
author of *Stay Woke: A Meditation Guide for the Rest of Us*

"*How to Break Up with Your Friends* shows the innate power of one of the most underappreciated relationships— our friendships—and gives a crystal clear map of exactly how to unlock that power."

MELISSA AMBROSINI
bestselling author of *Comparisonitis* and host of
The Melissa Ambrosini Show podcast

"*How to Break Up with Your Friends* puts the power of friendship front and center in a way most of us have never contemplated before. Now, more than ever, we need to do friendship right. Erin shows us how."

DENISE VASI
founder of Maed

"'Breaking up' with a handful of my girlfriends over the years were some of the most painful and yet also powerful experiences of my adult life. When I think of heartbreak, it's not the men I've dated that come to mind, but the friendships that had to end! I WISH I had had a guide as impactful as the one Erin Falconer has created here. Her fresh perspectives and approachable strategies form an excellent compass for navigating one of life's most complex journeys."

ERIN KING
author of *You're Kind of a Big Deal*

"*How to Break Up with Your Friends* is such a great reminder of not only the value of friendship but the personal responsibility a great friendship demands."

MANDANA DAYANI
creator and cofounder of I am a voter. and co-host of *The Dissenters* podcast

"A refreshing and relatable take on modern-day friendships. Erin shows us how to mine our myriad social connections to find the true gems."

FRANCINE JAY
author of *The Joy of Less* and *Lightly*

"*How to Break Up with Your Friends* is really about how (and why) to maintain important connections, and it's a blueprint for how to become a better friend yourself. Falconer tackles the subject of friendship with the seriousness it deserves, outlining the life-changing benefits of friendship (something I agree with wholeheartedly!). I plan on gifting this book to my dearest ones with personalized inscriptions."

GINA HAMADEY
author of *I Want to Thank You*

How To
Break Up
with Your
Friends

Also by Erin Falconer

How to Get Sh*t Done

ERIN FALCONER

How To
Break Up
with Your
Friends

Finding Meaning,
Connection, and
Boundaries in
Modern Friendships

sounds true
BOULDER, COLORADO

The wood used to produce this book is from
Forest Stewardship Council (FSC) certified forests,
recycled materials, or controlled wood.

Printed in Canada

BK06242

Library of Congress Cataloging-in-Publication Data

Names: Falconer, Erin, author.
Title: How to break up with your friends : establishing new boundaries
    for modern friendships / by Erin Falconer.
Description: Boulder, CO : Sounds True, 2022.
Identifiers: LCCN 2021018480 (print) | LCCN 2021018481 (ebook) |
    ISBN 9781683648130 (hardback) | ISBN 9781683648123 (ebook)
Subjects: LCSH: Friendship. | Interpersonal relations.
Classification: LCC BF575.F66 F433 2022 (print) | LCC BF575.F66
    (ebook) | DDC 177/.62–dc23
LC record available at https://lccn.loc.gov/2021018480
LC ebook record available at https://lccn.loc.gov/2021018481

10 9 8 7 6 5 4 3 2 1

*To all the girls
I've loved before*

Some people go to priests;
others to poetry; I to my friends.

Virginia Woolf

CONTENTS

INTRODUCTION

I bet you felt like an asshole for picking this book off the shelf.

An even bigger one for buying it.

And yet, notice how quickly you were drawn to it.

The truth is, I chose this title to get your attention, not because I think everyone needs to go through their contact list with a machete. While I certainly do believe, in a world of chaos and clutter, it is imperative to be discerning and thoughtful about just who you remove from your life, *it is at least as important to understand who you are keeping in your life and how to be better in those relationships and expect better from them.* But these days, no one is walking into a bookstore looking for a book about how to be a better friend.

And that's the problem.

We have accepted mediocrity in ourselves and in our friendships for far too long. And yet, nothing has more power in its ability to help give us fuel, inspire joy, and create true meaning than friendship. Friendships are highly impactful for women. And yet, despite priding ourselves on our big friend networks, I believe we are actually the biggest offenders in dialing in mediocrity. We're afraid to ask for what we really want and need, afraid to rock the boat—and in turn, live with friendships that often take more than they give. Today, so much of our time is curated (perfect Instagram feed, anyone?), and yet there seems to be so little thought about the people we keep in our lives. Why are we so tired and frustrated all the time? Well, let's start here, shall we?

Clichés surrounding female friendships try to limit what are actually complex, important relationships. The most damning of these is the notion of competition as an aspect of every female friendship—that we're all fighting over guys, or jobs, or other friends. The flip side to that "mean girl" trope is that female friendships are sugary trips to the spa—without any tension or conflict ever. This is a time of enormous potential for women—individually and collectively. We've learned through social justice movements that we're strongest when we support each other. It's so important that we create strong networks of friends in order to foster this potential. This isn't just about being liked; there is a real responsibility here. Sometimes, that means letting go of some of the relationships that aren't pulling their weight. It certainly doesn't mean that they didn't provide value along the way. They should be respected. But you don't owe them the rest of your life if, after careful consideration, you decide they aren't working any longer.

In researching this book, I found that in so many legacy friendships the participants could no longer remember what they actually liked about the other person. It seemed that their only motivation in keeping the relationship was to be liked, or rather, not to be disliked. When this is the motivation, the relationship has run out of gas or has been built upon faulty architecture. Being liked (or not disliked) should never be the goal. Rather, acting and being seen as authentically yourself, delivering and embracing genuine stewardship—and all the responsibility that entails—are far more worthy goals. And yet, they require courage and take so much more work that it is easy to see why choosing the default factory settings for friendship has become the norm. It is also easy to see, then, why some of our potentially most important relationships have become watered down. Suckers of energy, rather than givers.

I, myself, have a complicated relationship with relationships. In 2005, I lost my dearest friend in the world, Jocelyn, in the most shocking and horrifying way. Much was unclear in the days after, but what was totally clear was that I was left with a gaping hole in my heart that most surely could never be filled. The love and support of other friends were crucial at this time, but the only way I could survive was to numb myself and to accept that joy would no longer be a part of my life portfolio. I could feel happy, I could feel excited, but joy had left the building. This strategy worked for a long time. In fact, I don't know if I ever would have questioned it, until I found myself—actually the world found itself—in a bizarre and scary situation. Up until recently, if asked, I would have said I thought I was a pretty good friend. I make myself available for people in my life; I feel like I'm a good listener and give decent advice. I can be funny and daring and outspoken. However, I guess it took an event as extreme as my friend's death—a global pandemic, millions infected, hundreds of thousands dead, and stay-at-home quarantine orders for months and months—to jar me back to the truth: an understanding of what friendship really was, and what I had numbed away, all those years ago.

In the midst of my quarantine, eyeballing a "Zoom happy hour" invitation with irritation, I had a revelation. Why was I so annoyed that this person—my friend—longed to connect with me, having not seen me for months? It was in that moment, a moment I had felt numerous times over the past months, with various people, that I began to take stock. As I looked back, I also realized that there were certain people for whom I genuinely felt homesick; I really longed to see and sit with them and share. I started to look at each friendship in my life, and clear divides started to form between those I really didn't miss or feel the need to see at all and those whose presence in my life I missed. This isolation, this forced vacation from my friendships, while painful, irritating, and frankly scary, had given me an opportunity to reflect on the important people in my life and how these relationships were affecting me (and them). *Why hadn't I done this before? How could I allot such a significant amount of my most precious time to these relationships with so little analysis or reflection?*

Well, I would start now.

What I realized was twofold: (1) the huge value differential between the various friendships in my life that had gone unexamined, some for decades, and importantly, (2) how my own self-imposed numbness had crippled my ability to be a really *great* friend, despite all outward indicators to the contrary. In my attempt to avoid pain and reduce expectations, I had removed all of my vulnerability. I'm not alone—we live in a society that condemns any sort of vulnerability as weakness (as opposed to embracing the truth that real strength can only come from vulnerability). So, it's easy to see why I, and society at large, seem to have stepped away from the power of true friendship and enabling a complete human experience in favor of the far safer, 140-character-type exchange. Because the truth is, when you really start to examine your friendships, you have no choice but to examine yourself—who you really are, what you really want, *what you're really made of*; people these days are running, not walking, away from any time of deep self-reflection or intimacy with themselves, so how can we possibly be truly great in relationships?

And yet, what greatness lies on the other side of all that hard work.

Let's start with living longer lives (scientifically proven!). Living fuller lives. Feeling a greater sense of importance and influence. Feeling more loved. Feeling more love. Feeling more respected and heard. How about just feeling more? Having more fun. Creating more memories. The list goes on and on when you throw away indifference or playing it safe and really go for true, meaningful connection in friendships. So, I decided to give it a whirl and started by examining my "Zoom happy hour"–irritation friendship.

I started to realize I was very good friends with someone I wasn't very good friends with at all anymore. I'm not sure if that makes sense, but after reading that happy hour text from her, I felt a mixture of frustration and guilt from simply seeing her name on my screen. Upon further reflection, I'd been feeling that way for quite some time but had just been pushing these feelings further and further down. How had we gotten here? Was it just me? Was it her too? I realized I had been going through the motions for a long, long time. Furthermore, even if it had just been me going through the motions, there was no way the experience could have been fulfilling for her either, no matter which way you sliced it.

I was able to pinpoint the moment (years earlier!) when I believe all of this began. Living in Los Angeles, you have friends that live far away—maybe not by miles, but factoring in traffic, it can take me more than an hour of harrowing driving to see some of my friends. One of my really great friends lived on the exact opposite end of town, and so it was particularly difficult for us to meet. I began noticing that every time we were supposed to meet on my side of town, something always "came up" for her, and those plans were rarely kept. I remember talking in detail, over and over again, with a mutual friend about how annoyed I was. This mutual friend concurred that she had also been on the receiving end of what seemed like some selfish behavior. But strangely, I never brought it up directly with the friend in question. I found myself increasingly irritated every time I drove to see her, and so I gradually saw her less and less. She never stopped trying to set dates, however. In isolation, this was not necessarily a big problem—and from the outside looking in now seems like something that should have been pretty easy to address and resolve. But I didn't. So, my irritation about travel times now extended into many other channels of our friendship. I found myself waking up to the fact that we are not really friends at all, despite both of us espousing to all that we are the best of friends.

I had many questions, but what I was sure of was that I was left feeling frustrated and irritated by this relationship, instead of feeling nurtured and supported. Was this simply a legacy friendship that had run its course, and we had hung on too long? Or was this relationship a victim of the times? In the face of overscheduled schedules, busy lives with our priorities out of whack, allowing for too many things left unsaid and solvable problems left unsolved, had we turned something once great—a true friendship—into nothing more than an eye roll? A once great energy source into a great energy suck?

Finally, during quarantine, something profound happened: an eruption of understandable rage and hurt in the face of yet another unspeakable act of murderous violence against a Black person in the United States, with the killing of George Floyd. Weeks of unrest, peaceful protests, some protests invaded by violent elements, organizing, rethinking, and reassessing our values and behaviors. The impact on relationships of all kinds has been immeasurable. Each of us has had to confront with honesty the part we have played and are playing in perpetuating a system that values some people more than others. A personal inventory of our own contribution to systemic racism is necessary. This becomes particularly painful when examining the relationships in our own lives. How do we really treat other people? Are we hospitable and welcoming to people different from us? Or do we casually and narcissistically distance ourselves from anyone who challenges our power and status? Can we see flaws in past beliefs and actions and be willing to be accountable? As we'll explore throughout the book, it is imperative to have a variety of friends in your circle. But how do we do this in a way that is respectful and sincere and not in a way that perpetuates the problem we seek to overcome? More about the importance of these ideas as we move through the book. Regardless of the difficulty, it is obvious that we must find a way. Earnestly creating friendships that reflect our deeply held values is the way to move forward.

All of these questions prompted me to look at each one of my friendships—the people who took up a lot of my space (and I theirs). Perhaps what shocked me the most was that I had never considered doing this before. I wrote a whole book detailing how to critically analyze how you spend your time. There are diets that ask you to write down everything you eat to get a better handle on what you're consuming. Why shouldn't we think about our nearest and dearest more pragmatically? What if we did the work? Made the effort? Made a plan? Maybe if we took stock, our lives could be that much richer, that much more meaningful.

So that's what I did, and it has changed my life. With this book, I set out to try and take all of my learnings and condense them into the major categories I believe will help illuminate and inform the meaning, importance, practice, and ritual of what a good friendship can be. Just as every human is different, relationships are full of nuance and aren't one size fits all. So, I won't pretend there is a single formula that works, but I do believe there are beliefs and practices that can help shape your world, along with one of the most important aspects of that world—your friendships—to help create a life really worth living.

In this book, you will:

- Learn how to take stock of who is in your life, their role, and if the relationship is serving you (and them) in its current form.
- Learn how to treat yourself with respect, love, and kindness so you can model this for any current or future relationship.
- Clearly understand what your role and expectations are in each relationship, so you can understand the time and emotional energy you are expected to give to any one person at any one time.
- Understand the importance of nurturing good friendships and what the anatomy of a truly healthy, rewarding relationship looks like.
- Understand how your current views on friendship are based on your earliest friendships—and pivot around who you've become.
- Learn the critical value of rupture and repair within each relationship and how to stop fearing constructive confrontation.
- Learn how to deepen the friendships you're in, the ones that really matter, and how to have the tougher conversations for those that don't.
- Do a deep dive to understand the full spectrum of who you are and your personality type so you can create a friend profile for creating new friendships moving forward.

You grabbed this book *wanting*, *needing* to know how to set free what no longer serves you in friendship. And we will most definitely get to how to break up with your friends, but before we can contemplate that with any efficacy, we all must understand the astounding importance of modern friendship and how to be a truly great friend.

Certainly, no one can replace the best friend I lost. She was truly one in a million. But can there be other incredible friendships—sources of strength, love, and dare I say joy? If we are willing to put in the work; ask for what we want; and be honest, accountable, and vulnerable, then we have the power to tap into a greatness that only true friendship can unlock.

So, let's begin.

CHAPTER 1

Actually, You *Are* Here to Make Friends

The best time to make friends is before you need them.

ETHEL BARRYMORE

F riendships have always been essential to human survival and evolution. Of course, without some form of family unit, humans would not have continued as a species, but without social connection outside the family, we couldn't have evolved the sophisticated societies many of us live in now. Family and romantic relationships get most of the attention when it comes to analysis, study, observation, and support. And yet, unless you're in a reality show about you and your seventeen siblings, you almost surely have more friends than you do partners or immediate family. Perhaps the number and variety of our friends make friendship trickier to track.

Our very design makes us crave human contact. Belonging to a group improved humans' chances of survival. Ancient humans would groom each other (parents still groom their children) and receive an encouraging endorphin hit from that connectivity. Our bodies and brains were telling us, before we could consciously understand, that being with others is supposed to feel good and safe. As we evolved from small, nomadic hunter/gatherer groups to larger agrarian villages and then more permanent industrial societies, our bodies and brains continued to deliver that endorphin high from maintaining human connection. We feel well and happy when we have friends. Robin Dunbar of the University of Oxford is well known for his study of friendships. He posits that as we evolved from our ancient ancestors, we developed language and gossip as a much more scalable way to connect than actual touch. He says, "In the course of our human evolution, as we've been trying to evolve bigger and bigger groups to cope with the challenges the world has thrown at us, we needed some additional mechanism to allow us to break through what was essentially a glass ceiling." Gossip allows humans to "groom" several people simultaneously. It also helps us succeed in life, through collaboration and negotiation.

What's more, friends and close relationships can make a life worth living. More than just helping us survive, as we'll see below, friends have the power to help create meaning in our lives. When asked about the meaning of life in *The Meaning of Life: Reflections in Words and Pictures on Why We Are Here* (produced by *Life Magazine*) Pulitzer Prize–winning author Annie Dillard said:

> We are here to witness the creation and abet it. We are
> here to notice each thing so each thing gets noticed.
> Together we notice not only each mountain shadow
> and each stone on the beach but, especially, we notice
> the beautiful faces and complex natures of each other.
> We are here to bring to consciousness the beauty and

power that are around us and to praise the people
who are here with us. We witness our generation
and our times. We watch the weather. Otherwise,
creation would be playing to an empty house.

Friends Make You Healthy

There are few ways that friends *don't* add to your health.

In a 2016 review of several studies, Yang Claire Yang, a sociologist at the University of North Carolina–Chapel Hill, found that the higher degree of social integration people had, the lower their risk of negative health outcomes.

A late 1990s study conducted by Sheldon Cohen looked at the effect a large and diverse social circle had on the chances of a person catching a cold. More than two hundred healthy people were given a dose of rhinovirus. The larger and more diverse people's social network was, the less susceptible they were to the common cold, and the less virus they shed.

A large-scale Swedish study found that people with the fewest social connections were at a 50 percent increased risk of dying of cardiovascular disease. And should you get heart disease, friends help you recover. In a study by the *Journal of the American Heart Association*, patients with solid social support had better outcomes as well as fewer symptoms of depression.

To put it another way, your social connectedness has as much or more effect on your health and longevity as smoking cigarettes. Vivek Murthy, Surgeon General in Barack Obama's administration, recently published *Together: The Healing Power of Human Connection in a Sometimes Lonely World*. He wants us to look at loneliness in the same way we do hunger or thirst; it's a helpful sign that we need to address a problem. He writes, "The body's response from loneliness can be very helpful in the short term. But when those stress states become chronic, they begin destroying the body." And yes, the effects can be as negative as those of obesity or smoking.

Friends Make You Live Longer and Better

Neuroscientist Emily Rogalski leads a super-ager study at Northwestern University in Chicago. A super ager is defined as someone aged eighty years or older whose cognitive function is comparable to a person of middle age. This cohort remains physically and intellectually active. Rogalski finds that they are socially active as well. Strong social connections are believed to protect the brain in later life. Super agers have thicker cortices, are resistant to age-related atrophy, and have a larger left anterior cingulate—the part of the brain important to working memory and attention. "Different neurotransmitters are released when we feel compassion, empathy, love, and friendship," says Rogalski. Many of the people participating in Rogalski's study report having warm and trusted friendships.

Dean Ornish, who has studied the habits of people living in blue zones—geographical areas in which people have low levels of chronic disease and live longer than anywhere else in the world—says, "The time we spend with loved ones is the single most important determinant in how long and how well we live."

This is particularly important for women, considering that we typically live six to eight years longer than men.

The Loneliness Epidemic

Back when I was running two companies, LEAFtv and my *Pick The Brain* blog, I had little free time. I felt like I was running around all day producing content for LEAF and then would get home to burn the midnight oil with *Pick The Brain*. A big part of my business with LEAF was networking, and so on nights that I wasn't home, I was often out at a work event. Needless to say, I was exhausted.

Without thinking about it, I would easily cancel plans with friends or be relieved when they canceled with me, feeling that these kinds of meetings were superfluous or more "nice to have" as opposed to necessary. I felt like meeting up with a friend would make me more tired and throw a kink in the following day rather than potentially provide me more energy. What's more, because I was always using work as an excuse to get out of things, that is what became the primary focus of my conversations with friends. So even when we did manage to hang out, what was making me so tired would inevitably dominate the conversation. When I look back on this time of my life now, I feel like if I hadn't been so quick to axe those moments with friends, it could have really helped stave off my impending burnout and my growing sense of loneliness, despite having my days and nights filled to the brim.

Even with all the evidence of how much good friendships do for us, we still see them as a kind of luxury. If you've got an intense month ahead of you—a course to complete, a major deadline, a wedding to plan—it's likely that the first appointment to get deleted from your calendar is that happy hour with your girls. It just doesn't seem necessary when held up against professional pressure or family obligations. So, we cancel the coffee chats, the weekend hangs, and catch-up calls because it just feels like one more thing to get done. But we're paying a price for it.

According to a recent study by Cigna, a global health service company, nearly half of Americans feel alone, and two out of five Americans feel that their relationships are not meaningful. These numbers are higher than they were just a year ago. We're lonely.

Shasta Nelson, author of *The Business of Friendship: Making the Most of Our Relationships Where We Spend Most of Our Time*, says, "At the core of loneliness is that we don't feel like anyone knows us. You can even have a lot of close friends, but if none of your friends know what it's like to be you, you can feel lonely in an experience. Loneliness is not feeling seen and supported."

One of the key factors in feeling connected to friends is vulnerability. In order to call someone a good friend, you have to be willing to show your imperfections as well as accept theirs. In the era of social media, this is particularly important. Instagram, Facebook, and TikTok have a way of encouraging us to edit our lives. You want to upload a great shot from your holiday, when you were feeling rested and relaxed. You share a snap of your kid when her face is clean and her hair is brushed. You write a post about a big win at work. Of course, it's fun to share life's upsides. The effect, however, is that the way we represent ourselves is like an eclipse—we show only the shiny sliver, not the whole, messy truth of our lives. You might have hundreds of friends on social media, but the way we use those platforms is the opposite of intimacy. In my experience, even when moments shared on social media are less than perfect, too often these also feel like curated messages of messiness rather than the real deal. As a result, I feel like the pseudo-shares of intimacy are almost more misleading.

Murthy says that loneliness is deeply consequential. He has studied the far-ranging effects of social isolation. In speaking to people across the United States, Murthy was struck by the pervasiveness of loneliness and by the shame that surrounded it. He says, "I think part of the reason is that saying you're lonely feels like saying you're not likeable, you're not lovable—that somehow you're socially deficient in some way. The reality is that loneliness is a natural signal that our body gives us, similar to hunger, thirst. And that's how important human connection is." Responding to a feeling of loneliness by seeking connection is a healthy, human process. If we ignore it, we risk chronic stress and all the negative physical and emotional effects that come with it.

The importance of friendship to health is so great that many doctors and scientists are beginning to look at it from a public health lens. Just as a healthy diet and exercise have become more mainstream recommendations from doctors, it's likely that soon doctors will be prescribing socializing to their patients at their checkups.

Friendly Neighborhood Stress Busters

Five years ago, most of the queries I received via *Pick The Brain* were all about time management and productivity: *How can I get more done?* (hence my first book). But in the past couple of years, my inbox and comments have been dominated by questions such as: *How do I reduce anxiety? How can I feel less stressed?* In my experience, there has been a major shift toward impending burnout, fear, and stress. As we frantically search for answers, my belief is that at least some of the answers are often right in front of us. *Friends reduce our stress levels.* And diminishing stress is enormously beneficial to your overall health. Stress is associated with negative health outcomes in myriad ways, from your gums to your heart, and can make you more susceptible to everything from the common cold to cancer and diabetes, according to a review essay in the Association for Psychological Science's magazine, *Observer,* in 2007.

Here's how it works. In moments of stress, your body releases hormones—adrenaline, cortisol, and norepinephrine—that boost your heart rate, increase respiration, and increase the availability of glucose in the blood, all to enable the fight-or-flight response. In a moment of sudden danger, you'll be able to sprint away or flip a car off of your child. But this response requires a lot of energy from your body. To compensate, other physical processes, such as digestion, reproduction, physical growth, and some aspects of immunity slow or shut down. When stressful events are infrequent or pass quickly, the body resumes its equilibrium. Chronic exposure to those stress hormones affects normal function in your body and can result in sleep problems, heart disease, headaches, weight gain, memory and concentration impairment, depression, and anxiety. Traumatic events in early childhood can lead to some people becoming more sensitive and easily triggered by stress. It's as if each of us has a stress set point, unless of course we actively try to change it.

In some respects, the evolutionary journey to the modern world might be the very reason we experience so much stress. Stanford neuroendocrinologist Robert Sapolsky has studied stress in baboon troops and found that safety and increased leisure time in primates—including humans—transforms the useful fight-or-flight mechanism into pointless suffering and illness. Most of us are lucky enough to live our day-to-day lives without the threat of physical danger. We have evolved from avoiding saber-toothed tigers, but our stress response remains the same. The modern-day tiger is a mean boss, a whiny child, or an argumentative partner. And you don't just experience stress when your boss snaps at you; you get to relive that unpleasant encounter—and the stress—as many times as you choose to ruminate on it.

When you're feeling either intense or chronic stress, you might not feel fit for company. But times of challenge are when friends can help the most. A 1990 study of female college students asked them to complete a challenging math test. When they took the test on their own, their heart rates went up. When they were allowed to take the test with a friend? You know the result, right? The presence of a friend calms us down. Lindzi Scharf, an entertainment reporter, wrote movingly in the *Los Angeles Times* about needing to lean on friends after learning her newborn daughter, Evan, had a rare and incurable disease. "We spent time with family and friends, who may not have understood what we were going through but stood by us so we felt a little less alone. My husband and I carved out self-care as best we could. In my husband's case it was CrossFit; I turned to writing and having coffee with girlfriends."

I reached out to Scharf to ask her more about her experience. Her daughter's health needs are significant, and it must be hard not to be swamped by them. She's quick to give friends the latest on Evan. "I want people in my life to really know what's going on, but I also think it's important to have other conversations. Literally, I always say, 'Please tell me about anything else. I don't want to talk about mitochondrial disorder anymore!'"

Friends and Habits

The Framingham Heart Study has been following the residents of the city of Framingham, Massachusetts, since 1948, looking at hypertension and cardiovascular health. Much of what is known about heart disease and the effects of diet and exercise is based on it. The finding that hadn't been predicted was the way health, for better or worse, could be contagious. The researchers have found that one person in a community becoming obese raised the chances of their friends becoming obese by 57 percent. But the reverse is also true. If your friends eat a healthy diet and regularly exercise, you are more likely to follow suit.

Suzanne Higgs, a professor in psychobiology of appetite at the University of Birmingham, found that the presence of friends actually diminished people's ability to recognize their bodies' own cues, such as feeling full. We tend to eat like the people we eat with. This impulse to do as others do can be manipulated for good. In another study, Higgs placed posters in a cafeteria showing which side dishes were most popular. When a vegetable dish was listed at the top, more of that dish was ordered. Particularly when you're new to a situation, you'll be looking for cues about how to behave. Even when the posters were removed, the behavior remained. A new norm had been established.

You can bolster your goals by making conscious decisions about what kind of people you spend time with. I know it sounds a little ruthless, but that marathon training is going to feel so much more torturous if all your pals are partying like rock stars every night.

Friends Help You Grow

Every friendship is its own jigsaw puzzle. The way you fit together with one friend might look radically different from the way you fit with another. There's that pal who's up for anything and makes any social event the best night ever. A different friend is the one you call when you suspect you've screwed up royally because you know she'll give it to you straight. There's your cheerleader, whom you absolutely need to see before you head into a nerve-racking presentation. And it's possible that you are all three of those types of people for other friends. Our personalities are relational—friends bring out different aspects of our characters. When we have close and caring relationships with people, it gives us an opportunity to see the world through their eyes, thus growing our empathy and compassion. Having a diverse group of friends allows you to grow in a way that having a small and homogeneous social group cannot.

I Zoomed with an old colleague I've been friendly with over the years, Elise Loehnen, author and podcast host, about how she continues to be shaped by her relationship with her best friend, Sarah. She says, "I met my friend Sarah at boarding school. I was new, and she sought me out. It's not that she's not capable of having hard days, but she's a really bright light. Now we both live on the westside of L.A. That offers a lot of relief to me and a place to be myself without judgment. She pulls me toward positivity. Even in high school—not that we didn't kvetch and moan—but she'd always say, 'But isn't it kind of fun?'"

A phenomenon known as the Michelangelo Effect supplies more reason to be mindful of who we are closest to. This refers to the artist's observation that sculpting was the process of chipping away at stone to reveal its ideal form. In a 1999 study, Stephen Michael Digrotas found that when someone close to you sees you in the way you want to become—healthier, more productive, more upbeat, whatever the case may be—that relationship will have a positive effect on you, and it will help you become the person you want to be.

Friends Help Cocreate Who We Are

For me, all of the physical health and mental health benefits of friendship are incredible, but I think the true power lies in how good friends help us discover who we really are. Experts as far back as eighteenth-century astronomer Maria Mitchell explored the idea that we could "co-create each other and re-create ourselves in our friendship." The continued work and development of the quintessential friendships in our lives help us build toward our full potential. In other words, when you work to fortify your friendships and develop close, nuanced relationships, you are also simultaneously building your own personal strength and character. Aristotle, arguably one of the greatest thinkers of all time, talked often about the power of friendship, specifically as it pertained to the self. In *Answers for Aristotle: How Science and Philosophy Can Lead Us to a More Meaningful Life*, Massimo Pigliucci discusses Aristotle's belief that "friends hold a mirror up to each other; through that mirror they can see each other in ways that would not otherwise be accessible to them, and it is this mirroring that helps them improve themselves as persons." Perhaps this helps explain why today we shy away from deep relationships: *Are we afraid of what we might find in the mirror?* Regardless, it is imperative, at least for those interested in becoming the best versions of themselves, to dive deep into friendship as a means of self-exploration, awareness, and potential.

The bottom line is that self-discovery can fuel stronger relationships, but strong relationships can ignite the most important parts of ourselves.

For a long time after the death of my dearest friend, I was just kind of treading water. Trying not to drown. Bills were getting paid. Work was getting done. But there was no momentum. No flow. I was stuck. As I mentioned earlier, I had a ton of support from my existing friends, my family, and my partner, but all of those connections now came with a filter. I couldn't escape what had happened, and as a result it had a way of being woven into almost all of my interactions. As a creative person, I just couldn't fathom writing another word, and so while there was no imminent or obvious threat to my demise, looking back, I was slowly dying. It wasn't until a couple of years later (years!) that I was introduced to a friend of a friend who was a budding director. When we met, there was an immediate chemistry. Instantly, we were talking about films and commercials and music videos, our inspirations for our work. I felt creative again, if only for that moment of conversation. I left our meeting, and for the first time in a long time I felt alive. Over the course of the next few weeks, we texted and talked and finally decided we would do a project together, a short film. I was blown away. For nearly two years the idea of being creative had felt completely out of reach, even nauseating. And yet, now I was giddy. I could not wait to get started. Through this creative work, some of the best of my career, I began to put myself back together. But more than the work, the friendship saved me. I could be free of tragedy. I could be defined by something else, totally. I could be seen for just me, a creative person, by somebody else. And the more this person witnessed me as creative, the more creative I became, sinking deeper and deeper into my potential rather than my sadness. This was almost eighteen years ago, and this person is still today one of the best friends I've ever had. Not only did this friendship change my energy and my outlook but also it allowed me to bring something new and positive back to my existing relationships—a fresh start. Most importantly, it helped me discover a part of me that I'm certain would have lain dormant otherwise.

Across the board, scientists, philosophers, and psychologists all agree that close friendships improve your life physically, mentally, and emotionally. They make room for both growth and error. They are great teachers and great healers. Perhaps, more importantly, they just make us better people. I don't know about you, but I feel like we need the best of people right now. So, the next time you flippantly check a follower count or a like count on one of your profiles, I encourage you to spend at least that amount of time on a real relationship that has the power to transform you in every sense of the word.

"I will say there was one girlfriend who came to visit during our hospital stay. I totally thought all of that would scare off anyone who visited. It's too much for anybody. Every day we were there, there was some sort of emergency. So then to my surprise, at the end of her being there, she's like, 'Oh, what are you doing on Golden Globes night? We need to up your hospital bed game.' She just brought such a sense of positivity to being there.

She knew, because my husband and I both work in the entertainment industry, that the Golden Globes meant that he was going to be out working that night, and it would just be me alone with Evan. So, she came back on Globes night, and it was this night where we did not have time to watch anything on TV because it was actually a really heavy night. Thank goodness she was there with me. At one point, we needed to run to go get a stomach X-ray. Just all sorts of stuff was unfolding, and she was there, and she put on a brave face and made it seem like, 'Oh, everything about this is totally normal.'

I think, to me, that's friendship. To me, it was always that friendship would be people who aren't afraid of your darkness and vice versa. I always felt that way, long before being in this boat. I always wanted to have friends in my life where what was going on was never bigger than our bond. The fact that I think those are the kinds of friendships I've nurtured over the years, once I did find myself in this boat, people have been pretty incredible. I feel very lucky."

JOURNALIST LINDZI SCHARF

on her two-month stay in the hospital after her
daughter, Evan, was born with an incurable illness

CHAPTER 2

You Should Be Your Own Best Friend

Friendship with oneself is all-important, because without it one cannot be friends with anyone else in the world.

Eleanor Roosevelt

I f this is a book about friendships, why am I starting out by talking about you? Shouldn't we jump right into who your friends are, what you're getting from them, how to improve those connections, and who's got to go?

Don't worry, we'll get to all that. But before we dive into friendships, we have to start with ourselves. I'm not talking about self-love in the have-a-cup-of-chamomile-tea-and-a-bubble-bath way. (There is a place for that, just not here!) This is about really knowing yourself as a necessary starting place for great friendships. In fact, what I'm really asking you to do is to become your own best friend. And in doing so, you're going to unlock your superpower, both to give and to receive true friendship.

In my previous book, *How to Get Sh*t Done*, I talk about how we spend our time and how to be more purposeful about it. I—and many others—find it valuable to carefully consider where we put our energy, to be intentional rather than reactive to the vagaries of our hectic lives. I spent a lot of time analyzing all the ways women get pulled off course by doing too much and yet achieving too little of real value. I was noticing how absolutely drained a lot of women were feeling after allowing their schedules to become swamped. Through getting comfortable with pulling back from some seeming obligations, I had seen how much I could get done. And I was achieving *my* goals, not just saying yes to every request from the universe (and friends and family and colleagues).

Upon further consideration, I realized that a major element of our happiness, satisfaction, and wellness is *who* we're spending time with. Motivational speaker Jim Rohn is famous for his pronouncement that we are the average of the five people we spend the most time with. The truth is, we're affected by all the people we spend time with consistently. It only makes sense to be at least aware and at best purposeful in choosing relationships.

But before you can make clear-eyed choices about the people you'll share time and intimacy with, you have to know yourself. How can you possibly know which friendships should be cultivated and which can be allowed to fade away without knowing yourself, your values, your needs, your strengths, your weaknesses, and your goals? Simply, you can't.

Just like making reactive choices with your time, making those kinds of choices in friendships means you might end up with people around you who don't support you, don't respect you, and worst of all don't really see you. And vice versa. Or maybe it's not even as extreme as all that. Maybe you just don't connect in a lasting way.

I checked in with my good friend Jessie De Lowe, a manifestation expert and cofounder of the *How You Glow* blog, about the importance of caring for and understanding yourself because she has spent the better part of her career exploring how to unlock deeper parts of the self with her clients. She shared these wise words, which really resonated with me:

> Your relationship with yourself sets the tone for every
> other relationship in your life. We act as a mirror for
> one another, so if you are someone who often judges
> yourself, you are more likely to judge others as well
> as perceive judgment directed at you from others.
> Negative feelings about oneself and a lack of self-love
> interfere with one's ability to truly show up and be
> present in your relationships. When we make nurturing
> ourselves a priority and feel like our own cup is full,
> we have so much more to give, and in turn, can so
> much more freely receive. This balanced exchange
> of energy sets the tone for a healthy relationship.

When you know yourself and continue to check in with yourself about where you're at, how you're feeling, what you want, and so forth, you'll know where and with whom to place your energy and time.

So, how to start?

I Hear Voices (That's Okay, It's Just Me)

Let's be clear, most of us are far from being our own best friends. You might think of yourself as someone who has reasonably strong self-esteem. Objectively, you know that you're intelligent, hardworking, and kind. Maybe you're also funny or give great advice. Perhaps you have a flair for décor, or you bake a superb flourless chocolate cake. Even if you know that you have awesome qualities, you might still be a shitty friend to yourself. And here's where it shows: self-talk.

What-talk? Self-talk is the chatter that runs through our minds all day long. It can involve conscious thoughts or observations ("Oh, no, I forgot to rebook that dentist appointment!") and unconscious beliefs and biases we've collected over a lifetime ("Man, I suck at parallel parking!").

The self-talk most people allow to fill their minds is pretty nasty. Don't believe me? As a starting place, try simply observing your thoughts—don't try to change them yet. And pay particular attention to your thoughts when things go wrong. For example, you get stuck in traffic and arrive late to an important meeting. What goes through your mind? Do you tell yourself, "This is unfortunate—I really need to give myself more time in the future so I can arrive feeling calm and prepared"? Or do you go straight to, "I'm such an idiot. Who can't arrive on time? They all think I'm a loser"? Or imagine you find yourself too swamped with deadlines to make it to your spin class for two weeks running. When you think about it, what goes through your mind? Is it, "This is a stressful time, and the last thing I need to do is to beat myself up about what I'm *not* doing. Next week, I'm going to get back to the gym, and I know it will decrease my stress big time"? Or do you go something like this? "Well, here come the pounds! I can never stick to anything. Why even bother?" What if it's a scenario where you haven't even done anything yet? You notice a new job opening in your company. It's a pretty big jump up from where you are now, but you've been working your ass off, and it's been forever since you've had a raise or a promotion. Do you encourage yourself? "I've gained a lot of skills; my manager regularly relies on me to go above and beyond, and she should want to keep me motivated and excited." Or is it more like, "No one will ever see me as a senior player. Seriously, who do I think I am?"

In *The Three-Word Truth About Love and Being Well*, Clark Falconer (my dad!), a psychiatrist, writes about the power of the words we choose. "We know for certain now that the way we think changes everything. Our words are sources of light and energy, darkness and pain, and as soon as we think something, it begins to happen. Yet most people stay stuck in lower consciousness. They don't tap into the vast energy available to them in higher consciousness simply because they misunderstand and misuse words and their associated feelings."

In other words, you can choose the way you think about things, and it does make a difference to how you feel. In the words of Henry Ford, "Whether you think you can or can't, you're right." None of this is to say that life doesn't throw up actual roadblocks—and some of us have more roadblocks than others—but that within the space you have to alter your reality through your own thoughts, it's worth making that effort.

Make note of your self-talk for just a week. How would you characterize your inner voice? Is she encouraging? Compassionate? Does she see complexity and nuance in your life and choices? Or is she nasty? Is she a friend or foe? If you're having trouble deciding what kind of "person" your inner voice is, here's a surefire way of figuring it out. Can you imagine your actual best friend uttering the things you say to yourself? If you called your closest friend after a disastrous presentation at work, what would she say? "Well, you fucked up again. What were you expecting? You're just not that talented." Uh, I certainly hope not. Isn't it more likely that she'd say something along the lines of, "Oh, man, that sounds awful. I'm so sorry. I bet it's not quite as bad as it's feeling right now. And even if it wasn't your very best work, everyone knows you're amazing, and no one is going to hold that shit against you. Want to meet for a drink?"

If that's not giving you a clear enough picture, think about how you speak to your best friend. Do you tell her she's stupid, fat, lazy, or useless? Again, I certainly hope not.

Why does it matter how we talk to ourselves? Because we're talking about an internal dialogue, who cares if we're a little (or a lot) rough on ourselves? It turns out we should all care. Brené Brown is known, among many other things, for her groundbreaking work on shame. After studying thousands of pieces of evidence over six years, Brown arrived at a few key ingredients to creating meaningful connections. It's widely understood that the essence of friendship is seeing and being seen. So, in order to make authentic attachments with others, we must allow ourselves to be truly seen. It makes sense, right? If you're always fronting a false version of yourself, even if people are drawn to you, your relationship will be weak and inauthentic. Real friendship relies on both parties showing up as themselves, warts and all. And why might we not show up as ourselves? Well, if we buy what that negative self-talk is constantly telling us, we're likely to believe that our true selves are unworthy. If you have the notion, at the core of your beliefs, that you aren't worth much, why would you put that on display? You likely wouldn't. And if you hold back from being authentic, you'll never have meaningful connections.

And that's how we go from knowing lots of people—hello 750 Facebook friends!—to owning a swimming-pool-sized hole in our hearts called loneliness.

In looking at what distinguishes people able to make real connections from those unable to, Brown found that the key variable was self-worth. When we have self-worth, we have courage to be vulnerable, compassion for ourselves and others, and willingness to be authentic in relationships. Brown calls people with these qualities "wholehearted."

What strikes me most about that word is the idea that most of us are walking through life half-hearted or maybe even quarter-hearted. We're so afraid of vulnerability that we do anything to distance ourselves from it. As Brown observes, we are the most in debt, obese, addicted, and medicated cohort in history. She goes on to point out that this numbing isn't selective. If you're drinking/shopping/eating to avoid difficult emotions, the unfortunate door prize is a numbing of positive emotions, too, such as gratitude and joy.

So, how do you turn around your self-talk and become a better friend to yourself? A series of studies in 2014 came up with an ingenious answer: Talk to yourself by name. I know, I know, it seems eccentric at best and wildly narcissistic at worst. In these studies, researchers found that people whose self-talk included "I" and "me" experienced more social anxiety, regret, and shame. Those instructed to call themselves by name were able to do what scientists call "self-distancing." It's exactly what it sounds like. Self-distancing allows you just enough space in your thoughts to see situations with a cooler head and a kinder heart. Self-distancing gives people the chance to check some of those gut-level biases and beliefs against reality. ("Is Erin *really* the stupidest person in this meeting? Probably not. Okay, carry on.") These people experienced less shame and anxiety, even after completing challenging tasks such as giving a speech in front of an audience.

The flip side of using this kind of self-talk is naming that unpleasant inner voice as a way of taming that beast. Brown calls the voices gremlins. Psychotherapist Carissa Karner calls the voice her inner mean girl. Naming your inner nag, mean girl, taskmaster, or hater is also a way to take away the sting of the things she's telling you.

I've allowed my own inner mean girl to create tension with a friend. It seems like a particularly easy ditch to drive into with a friendship that has become less solid. It's so easy for that friend to become the scapegoat for your own, unresolved personal problems. I have a good friend who has a different life from mine. She doesn't really work, or at least not in the traditional sense of a nine-to-five job, and she doesn't have children, so between these two things, she seems to have a lot more free time than I do. She is wildly creative, interesting, funny, and generally a joy to be around, but I noticed, with my recent increased self-reflection, that I had growing frustration with her. This time, I was neck deep into writing this book and *way* behind on my deadline (one of the great casualties of COVID-19 with no child care was my ability to work on this book), and so the pressure was really on. As I was well into a thought, my phone rang, and I saw this friend's name on my display. I was immediately hot with frustration: "Why is she calling me in the middle of the day? She knows I have this deadline! Of course, she doesn't *actually* know what that means!"

I had done this many times before, but this time I caught myself.

Here I was, denigrating this person (and the relationship)—she had probably simply called to say hi, check in, or tell me a funny story—because of something that was entirely my problem. I was super stressed, tapped for time, and on the brink of dropping the ball (or at least that was the negative narrative I had playing on repeat in my head). Also, I had to admit that I was feeling a lot of anxiety and insecurity about being my family's breadwinner and about whether I could keep us all afloat. And I had some jealousy that money doesn't seem to be an issue for her. In my mind, she "had it easy." Again, my stuff, not her stuff. But instead of dealing with all that, I projected my anxiety outward and let my friendship be the punching bag. As I looked at my behavior to see if it extended out to anyone else, I was surprised to see that at moments it had. What I also realized was that my behavior bounced right off the really solid friendships (not an excuse to continue doing it!). But the friendships that had problems absorbed this behavior, and, as a result, the relationships suffered. So, in this example, there are two findings: (1) I was projecting my own personal angst and fear onto the relationship, to no good end, and (2) I clearly had some unresolved issues with my friend that I needed to look at. So, I needed to do some more work to get to the bottom of these unresolved issues. It was clear that I needed a much higher awareness of my negative processes and self-care to deal with my shit so that I didn't take it out on my relationships. If I couldn't be a friend to myself, I couldn't expect to be a great friend, period.

The pinnacle of self-talk is having compassion for yourself. Even though your inner mean girl isn't doing you any favors, she is trying to protect you. As Karner insists, accepting our inner mean girl is part of becoming our own best friend. The biases and beliefs our inner critic holds were likely gathered in childhood and likely no longer apply. Although she's just trying to protect you from failure or humiliation, a little distance from her will reduce your reactivity as well as quiet her.

Paying Attention

Most of us think we know ourselves pretty well by the time we hit adulthood. We've had enough experiences, romantic relationships, friendships, and possibly even jobs to know how our minds and hearts operate. Except we don't. At least, we don't know ourselves as well as we think we do.

In fact, blind spots in our self-knowledge can lead to poor decision making, emotional and interpersonal problems, and even decreased life satisfaction. In Jane Austen's tour de force *Emma*, the heroine starts as a master of self-delusion. Emma Woodhouse is clever, quick-witted, and highly judgmental. She imagines she knows what's best for everyone around her. In one of her first missteps, Emma encourages her less-sophisticated new friend Harriet to deny her feelings for a local farmer. Emma instead pushes her toward an ambitious young vicar. Not only does the manipulation end up hurting Harriet but also Emma begins to doubt her presumed omniscience. The book is filled with Emma making more mortifying blunders, but Austen's ultimate theme is the value of self-knowledge and reform. After Emma realizes the errors in her sense of self, she begins to see things as they truly are and develops deeper friendships (and lands Mr. Knightly).

In an article published in 2013, Erika Carlson of Washington University–St. Louis looked at the way mindfulness can improve our self-knowledge. Carlson asserts that the two key barriers in real self-knowledge are (1) informational—meaning we don't have accurate information about ourselves, and (2) motivational—we rely on ego-protecting assumptions about ourselves. Mindfulness—defined as the nonjudgmental observation of ourselves and our thoughts—allows us to see ourselves in our totality, with less fear and anxiety.

Now, before it sounds like mindfulness is a way to let yourself off the hook for your less-desirable qualities, it is not. Think of getting to know yourself via mindfulness as creating a baseline of data. You are likely to learn things about yourself that you don't love. For example, your anger flares when a friend is even five minutes late for a coffee date, or you have zero patience with your kids when you're hungry, or you feel rejected when a friend doesn't ask the right questions during a phone call. But think of it this way: you're having those reactions whether you acknowledge them or not. If you can train yourself to create a practice of nonjudgmental observation—mindfulness—then you've got some information to work with. Start this process with a sense of curiosity. If you don't want to have those reactions in your life, what could you do differently?

Could you ask your friend to text you when she's leaving home so you can time your own arrival to the café accordingly? Could you take care to regulate your blood sugar so *hanger* doesn't take over parenting? Could you let your friend know what's on your mind rather than waiting for her to ask you the right questions? Maybe and maybe not. But knowing yourself better and making choices puts you in greater control of how you behave and how you feel.

Building the ability to notice your thoughts and feelings is like developing any other skill—it takes time and practice. Ultimately, you want mindfulness to be something you come back to throughout your day, but you can start with five to ten minutes of it.

A lot of busy, high-functioning type A personalities (like me!) fear that mindfulness means the ability to clear your mind—which feels like an impossible task. But an empty mind is not the goal. What you're working toward is five to ten minutes (set an alarm so you don't have to check the clock) where you can sit quietly and focus on your breath. When you notice thoughts coming into your mind—and they will—don't worry about it; just note them, and bring your attention back to your breath. Your mind will wander again, offering up a buffet of all your worries and past failures. Watch them like a movie rather than getting caught up in the plot. And bring your attention back to your breath. That's it. (There are many other ways to meditate and to practice mindfulness, but this simple starter kit will get you going.)

The benefits of mindfulness are well documented and wide ranging. In 2011, Daphne M. Davis and Jeffrey A. Hayes of Pennsylvania State University amalgamated a mountain of research into the health and emotional results of mindfulness. Included were emotional regulation; decreased reactivity; increased response flexibility; improved interpersonal relationships (with others); and, most importantly for this chapter, improved intrapersonal relationships (with ourselves).

Because of the neuroplasticity of human brains, regular mindfulness actually alters the physical structure and operations of our brains. Mindfulness promotes brain growth in the regions that affect attention, sensory processing, increased information processing speed, and decreased task effort. Mindfulness is known to reduce anxiety and depression. And for the purposes of this chapter and getting to know yourself, one of the most important benefits of mindfulness is the way it develops empathy, compassion, and self-compassion.

The more you practice mindfulness, the easier it becomes. It's still a good idea to find ten minutes in your day to sit quietly and bring your attention to your breath, but you can move into mindfulness at any time by bringing your focus to only what you're doing. In a recent episode of Dan Harris's *10 Percent Happier* podcast, he recounted a story from an ER doctor who said that as she scrubbed her hands before operating, she used those few minutes to calm her mind, feel the water running over her hands, and allow the rest of her day's concerns to fall away.

I laughed out loud when talking to my psychology colleague and very good friend Jette Miller on how important mindfulness is. "It should be more important to have a cute nervous system than anything else!" she said emphatically:

> I find that in this culture, people are often waiting for a crisis—physical symptoms from stress or unhappiness—to change their behavior. Coming from Europe, I feel that there is a far greater attunement with oneself, care for oneself. For me, I consciously connect, really connect to myself through nature and music. And I pay attention to my body. How do I feel physically? What is my body telling me? It's not just like, "Oh, I have a headache, let me take a pill." I want to know what's going on emotionally, environmentally. What might this symptom be telling me?

She then went on to say something really interesting as it pertains to our friendships: "You have to try and regulate yourself through this type of mindful behavior; you can't just dump everything on a friendship. You have to have done the preliminary work yourself. Of course, you want to be able to share what is going on with you with a close friend; it's necessary for the friendship, but that is for support, not to process your material for you."

I want you to enjoy all the mindfulness-related benefits listed above. Who doesn't want to be less anxious, more creative, and more focused? But the real reason I want you to incorporate mindfulness into your day is it creates a time for you to be with you, for you to become adept at tuning in to your thoughts and feelings. This will help you get to know yourself, treat yourself with more kindness, and make you aware of what makes you feel good and what does not. And those are essential skills for developing great friendships.

Boundaries

So much has been written and discussed about romantic and family attachments that after a few missteps, most of us know where we stand on boundaries in those relationships. You feel good about calling your parents once a week, but the daily texts from them can grate. If the person you've been dating for nine months still wants to see other people, I'm pretty sure you have a stance on that.

But boundaries in friendships are much less clear. There simply hasn't been the same amount of analysis—either in social science or in pop culture—for you to have that same sense of knowing how you feel about them.

If you don't have standards for what you'll accept and what you won't accept in friendships—because you believe friendships should come naturally, without any effort—you can count on getting into trouble. Whether it's intentional or innocent, at some point a friend is going to cross a line with you. Maybe she brought a date to your dinner party without warning you. Maybe she forgot to ask you how that job interview went. Maybe she owes you money and never brings it up. For some people, those examples would be infuriating relationship enders. For others, they would not be a big deal. And of course, we want our best friends to know us well enough to anticipate what might hurt us. But if we're not willing to assert boundaries, then we can't expect friends to respect them.

Feeling entitled to boundaries requires self-respect. If we believe we have worth, creating reasonable boundaries feels, well, reasonable. If we don't feel good about ourselves, then boundaries might seem self-indulgent or even risky. What if we assert a boundary and our friends don't feel like we're worth the effort?

A couple of years ago, I was in the process of thinking about starting a new political company with a couple of partners. We moved fast and met a lot of interesting people who were all on board to help. I'll never forget the day I met one woman, in particular. She was sharp as hell, dressed like a million chic bucks and oozing confidence. I immediately wanted to be her friend and set out to do so. She seemed to like me, too, so shortly we were texting and meeting for coffee or drinks, all kind of centered around the business but ultimately forming a friendship. Eager to please, I was 1,000 percent accommodating: I would send out the call invites, I would make the reservations, I would do all of the following up. I was happy to be so useful (and hopefully impressive). About a year later, I felt a nagging, irritating feeling starting to emerge every time I thought about this friend. I started to look at the patterns in the relationship, and my behavior was clear. I obviously felt some deep-seated insecurity about my own self-worth and what I was bringing to the table. I tried to overcompensate by being so amenable, hoping she would never see how truly far beneath her I was. This manifested itself in me accepting behavior I never would have otherwise, being okay with my texts not being returned, being fine with her showing up thirty minutes late. To be clear, I created that behavior because I allowed it—because I had a negative script running in my head about how cool and successful this person was and how, compared with her, I wasn't. Now, I consider myself a fairly confident person by all measures, so if I can easily slip into this type of scenario, it's not difficult to see how someone really in the habit of beating themselves up can, time and again, slip into these exhausting roles of people pleasing. Needless to say, this new friendship of mine was doomed from the start. But it certainly didn't have to be.

It's not possible to create a comprehensive list of areas in which you must create boundaries because everyone has different issues they really care about. Boundary hotspots might be time, money, attention, reciprocity, trust, discretion . . . I could go on and on. Your job is to know what yours are. You don't do yourself or your friends any favors by acting like you're an anything-goes kind of person. No one is. It might feel awkward at first, but you're far better off finding kind ways of communicating your boundaries. The people who can't respect them aren't going to be great friends in your life, and the ones who do should get the best of you.

HOMEWORK

It might seem like you're taking the long way around to getting to better friendships, but taking care of yourself to build your own voice, self-worth, and self-respect are not only the keys to feeling better generally but also to bringing and modeling strength and compassion for those we love.

- Find five minutes a day for a mindfulness practice. Yes, *you do* have five minutes for this. There are lots of apps such as Calm or Headspace. Or take a device-free walk. Find a quiet space to daydream. Breathe deeply during your hot shower in the morning!

- Write down three to five examples of self-talk. How many are negative? How many are positive? How many have you checked to see if they are actually true? Start using your own name in your self-talk. Give your negative self-talk identity a name.

- Be nice to yourself. Treat yourself the way you'd treat your best friend. Write out three positive things you could say to yourself each day. And say them.

- Take a personal inventory of three to five of your own friendship strengths. Are you a good listener? Do you enjoy making your friends laugh? Are you super thoughtful?

"I met a good friend of mine in the water in Tel Aviv. Both floating in the water. Just casual, floating.

We became instant friends, hung out all the time. Texting all the time. We were both single. Both Russian-Israeli. We both had the same background. We became really good friends. For years! Then, I don't know what happened, but she left for New York and completely dropped me. No explanation. Vanished. I ran into her back in L.A., and she ran away from me. Literally. It was at Erewhon. I remember calling a mutual friend and being like, 'I just had the weirdest experience of my life.' She literally couldn't get away from me fast enough.

I racked my brains. I don't know what it is. I genuinely, I don't know what it is. What made her drop me?

I think for a while I was sad. I made excuses: 'Well, she moved to New York, so it's kind of like out of sight, out of mind.' But it was more than that. I could tell she didn't want anything to do with the friendship.

I went over and over in my head what I could have done. And there was just one possible instance. But I don't even know if this could be it. *This is the most L.A. story ever*. She came back from a trip to New York and wanted to have lunch, and we went to lunch at Angelini.

We had just sat down to lunch, and Chris Pine walks in right after. She knows the randomest actors, and she knew him well. She waves hi and you know, hugs and kisses, and he's like, 'Can I join you guys?' I was like, 'Sure!' And there's no fucking way I'm having lunch with Chris Pine and *not* going to get a photo. So, I had them take a photo of us, and I literally never heard from her again afterward. Not once. It's the only thing I can think of—she didn't like that I asked for a photo with Chris Pine.

She didn't say anything. That's the last time I saw her in a friendly context. I'd say that was three or four years ago. Then I ran into her at Erewhon. She couldn't run away fast enough."

JENNA

on being ghosted by a close friend/the Chris Pine effect?

CHAPTER 3

First Friendships

Little girls are cute and small only to adults. To one another they are not cute. They are life sized.

Margaret Atwood

I'll never forget my transition from sixth to seventh grade. I had gone to an all-girls private school since kindergarten. In seventh grade (first year of middle school), the school district opened up enrollment to include a whole slew of new students—many of whom had gone to public school before. There was a revived energy to my class and an obvious group of new, cool girls in my world. I was intimidated. Despite the uniform, these newcomers had style honed from years with no dress code and, way more importantly, the Holy Grail: *boy experience*. Immediately, I set my sights on being part of this cool new set.

I took on a new persona: always available, always nice, always humorous. I was able to get in with the new crowd, but it didn't take long before I started feeling like a trained monkey. I was on edge, never sure how I was going to impress them next. Over the course of a couple of years, it began to wear on me. What I didn't stop to think about at the time was why I felt like the nonperforming me wasn't enough. After all, I was the girl who had the lay of the land. I knew all of the students and teachers. I was class president of Grade 6 and already popular. If anything, these new girls were coming in not knowing anyone and not knowing what to expect. Instead, I set up a dynamic of people pleasing at the expense of my own happiness. As a result, the rules of our relationships (set by me) were bound for disaster. After I got too tired and frustrated to continue performing, my insecurity mounted, and my new friendships ended. Of course, as only a teen girl can serve up, they ended . . . *dramatically.*

After the breakup with that new friend group, I became good friends with a couple of girls who were smart and cool-ish. Most importantly, they were supportive. Among them, I was the star. I was my opinionated, brash, and sassy self, and they hung on my every word. I had gone from being the people pleaser to the pleased, and it felt great.

I can trace my people pleasing pattern throughout my life. Remember my story from chapter 2, when I sabotaged the budding friendship I had made through work by going out of my way to accommodate my friend and be boundary free? It feels like textbook me, circa the early 1990s, trying to keep the cool kids happy. When I look back, I find I take on this role often. The real question remains: Is it the best pattern for me? Clearly not. Those early friendships left a scar on me that affects my current relationships. What I've learned—and it turns out research supports this distinction—is the difference between popularity and friendships. Popular girls—or women—might have many people around them but not enjoy close relationships. Only now, after recognizing this pattern, do I understand how to tweak my existing friendships to create a more robust union—not built on angst or neurosis but rather true feelings and connection.

Childhood is a strange and dramatic time. What happens in our early years has an enormous impact on the rest of our lives, from our childhood economic status to how we were parented to what our school experience was like, of course. Right up there in the influence game are our childhood friendships. Those friendships come with inside jokes, shared secrets, common foes, and feelings that aren't romantic but do include love. Just as early family relationships set our standards for future partners and children, early friendships establish our expectations for future friendships. And yet, childhood is the time when we have the least control and say over how that looks. Early friendships help us learn sharing, empathy, and collaboration. But they can also teach us envy, manipulation, and bullying. When kids are young, their friendships almost entirely spring up from the peer group to which they have proximity: schoolmates, neighbors, and/or family friends. And as a culture, we really don't give young kids a lot of choice. There's a strong cultural norm to expect kids of the same age to get along. After we reach adulthood, it's much easier for us to design a life in which we spend as much time as possible with people of our choosing. This makes childhood not only a time of great learning but also one that can be rife with drama.

What's more, when you are young, you are still putting together who you are. According to neuroscientist and coauthor of *Welcome to Your Child's Brain* Sandra Aamodt, your brain is still developing until long past the teen years: "The car rental companies got to it first, but neuroscientists have caught up and brain scans show clearly that the brain is not fully finished developing until about age 25." If you're not fully cooked until twenty-five, imagine how impressionable a small child is. Important moments that happen at a young age have the power to transform who you become, and this certainly applies to how you develop through or are affected by your early friendships. They literally can change your trajectory. When Sasha Tong, a TV producer and cohost of the *What's Your Drama* podcast, arrived in Canada, she was a small-for-her-age girl from Hong Kong with a British accent (a result of Britain's history with Hong Kong). She skipped kindergarten and was placed in the first grade at five years old:

> I had a horrible first-grade teacher. She wouldn't let
> me go to the washroom. And then one day I peed. So,
> it's my first week in Canadian school. Think about
> that—it could have been social suicide. I could have
> become the *pee girl* for my whole life. But somehow,
> I was rescued by this sassy, little, precocious, very
> popular girl, Sarah Clarke. She took me under her
> wing, and we were friends all through elementary
> school and even into high school. She was the type to
> say, "I'm going to make you my friend!" So, I always
> think that if I had not had her . . . who knows what
> would have happened. But it changed the trajectory of
> my friend group and my confidence and everything.

It has long been believed women are better at the soft skills friendship requires. Socialization has a lot to do with that, but so do our brains. In *Forever Friends*, a book she coauthored with Christine Borzumato-Gainey, Suzanne Degges-White, a counselor and professor at the University of Northern Illinois, explains that even in the womb, girls are building what she calls the "friendship-ready brain." Through a combination of hormones, peptides, brain growth, and neural pathways, girls' brains are prepared to handle the tasks of communication, reading emotions, understanding social nuances, and nurturing others. The book goes on to say: "Girls enter the world better equipped to observe and remember emotional details. They are able to comprehend the nonverbal components of communication, including vocal tone, facial expressions, and body language to assess meaning more successfully than males."

Not surprisingly, children's ability to make friends and handle the ups and downs of friendships is influenced by their connection to their primary caregiver. British psychologist John Bowlby revolutionized the study of child development by introducing the concept of attachment theory. Children raised by loving, attentive caregivers learn that they are worthy of loving relationships and are considered to have a secure attachment. These children are more confident about striking up new friendships and likely have a standard for how they'll expect to be treated. On the flip side, children whose attachment to their caregiver is insecure—as a result of unpredictable or inattentive parenting—have fewer social abilities and might self-isolate or become aggressive.

This is not to say that kids who had a rough start can never have meaningful friendships, only that they will have to learn how to fit in with friends through trial and error.

Some of us lived with other people who affected our friendship skills: siblings. In *Forever Friends*, Degges-White and Borzumato-Gainey describe a study that showed that kindergarten teachers rated children with at least one sibling as having significantly higher interpersonal skills and self-control and having fewer behavioral problems than only children. She goes on to say that children with siblings do better at forming and maintaining friendships, getting along with different people, expressing feelings, and being sensitive to the feelings of others. Many people reading this will be thinking back to the vicious sibling wars of their childhoods and think, *What*?! But those battles actually gave you important practice in negotiation and conflict resolution.

One of the most dramatic and memorable passages in Louisa May Alcott's *Little Women*, the story of the four March sisters, is the battle between tomboy Jo and spoiled Amy. Jo and her sister Meg have been invited by handsome neighbor Laurie to the theater, and Amy desperately wants to join. Jo insists that Amy is too young and may not come, and Amy vows to get revenge. Knowing how to wound Jo best, she tosses Jo's handwritten manuscript in the fire, destroying it. When Jo discovers what Amy has done, she flies into a rage and declares she will never forgive Amy. Jo bears a grudge against Amy until the younger sister nearly drowns when she falls through the ice on which Jo and Laurie are skating. At the prospect of nearly losing her sister, Jo forgives Amy's horrible act.

I feel like I won the sibling lottery with my brother, Harris. We get along famously now, and have for a long time, but it wasn't always like that. When we were young, my brother and I used to really fight. Not all the time, but when we did, wowza! I'm talking hitting and screaming. (He's a redheaded Scorpio, and I'm a stubborn Capricorn who can't ever admit she's wrong, so the die was pretty much cast.) I felt like, being older, I always got the blame, and this really stung. I'm not sure what the turning point was—maybe when I started to assert my own voice with my parents, around age eight or nine? Eventually, I figured out that my brother could be an ally instead of an enemy. I figured out, or maybe we did it collectively, that we were better off together, and so from quite a young age I had a partner in crime. I learned something deeply important from this relationship that I feel I carry with me today. This idea of partnership, such as how we can be a team and get things from life together (not material things, but experiences). Being clear on a person's value and value to you (and vice versa) has really helped my relationships in life, and I attribute this to growing up with my brother. I don't know yet if I'll give my son a sibling. And if I don't, I know I need to give him lots of opportunities to mix it up with other kids to learn those skills.

Another building block necessary for kids to have success in friendships is a notion known as *theory of mind*. Theory of mind describes the ability to attribute mental states, such as thoughts, feelings, and desires, to others and to use this understanding to predict and explain behavior. For instance, Emily can understand that her friend Cecile is in tears because a doll has been ripped from her hands and can comfort her friend or try to help her get the doll back. As a child gets older, this theory of mind can become increasingly sophisticated, giving her more and better friendship skills. Having a strong theory of mind has been associated with the ability to discuss emotional states, which in turn is associated with maintaining positive and intimate connections, understanding other points of view, and reciprocity. All of which is to say, the better your understanding of human emotions is, the more likely you are to have great friendships.

Childhood friends—and how homogeneous or heterogeneous they were—laid a foundation for your ability to accept and tolerate new people throughout your life. Anna Cho, a psychotherapist (who also happens to be my internship supervisor), says, "If you're stuck with a certain comfortable network when you're young, you're going to be impacted later when you're in a different environment. That's shocking to the system, and then your potential is going to regress." She encourages kids not only to be in diverse social situations but also in ones that might make them uncomfortable. "Say a child is interacting with someone with autism. It's going to be a learning curve for them, but then they have expanded their capacity and tolerance and awareness so much so that many other individuals and personality styles still fit right in that grey area," she says.

Diversity in friendships can also be a saving grace when it comes to the minefield of middle school—the prime time for mean girl action. (Although some girls might have guy friends, research shows that same-gender friendships are the norm until well into high school.) Lindsay Sealey, in *Growing Strong Girls; Practical Tools to Cultivate Connection in the Preteen Years*, advocates steering girls away from intense best-friend-forever (BFF) friendships and toward multiple-friend circles. Ideally, she says, girls should have friends at school, friends they meet through activities or teams, family friends, and neighborhood friends. Not only does this expand their capacity for getting along with different people but also it means that drama with one person in this network isn't the end of the world.

A 2015 study looked at how social networks affect children, and it supports Sealey's advice. The researchers found that kids with a large network of friends benefitted by having many different kinds of experiences. They got a lot of practice in social skills and became more confident. Even kids with less than desirable traits, such as aggression, benefitted from large friend networks because they had the opportunity to receive corrective feedback from peers. These can be subtle but significant exchanges. A kid who always interrupts might notice that other kids are pulling back from her, and she might try to let other people finish their sentences. The bottom line is that friendship muscles grow with exercise, and if you build them in childhood, they'll take you into adulthood.

A 1998 study found that having friends in childhood has been shown to lead to high self-worth in adulthood. The same study, however, also found there was not the same clarity about peer-rejected or friendless kids. Kids who didn't have friends seemed more likely to be depressed adults, but their friendlessness was not predictive. All of that is to say that if you were a loner as a child, you are not doomed to be a sad and lonely adult.

Lainey Lui, founder of the Lainey Gossip website, television host of *The Social* and *Etalk* and cohost of the podcast *What's Your Drama*, was a loner as a child. She was the only child of immigrants who moved frequently—a scenario that had her feeling like an outsider much of the time. "I was shy. One of my memories is that at recess, often I'd just be by myself. There was a meadow next to our school, and I'd imagine things in the meadow and play different characters. I was super into Chinese soap operas then, and I would sing my Chinese songs to myself and re-enact the scenes that I really loved."

Those years as a loner meant Lui was slow to pick up some of the friendship skills she'd eventually have. She says she didn't know how to be a good and supportive friend in her teens and early twenties. "I have been a bad friend and have had to learn through losing friendships what those mistakes were." She came to realize that it's not about never making mistakes but learning how to face them, atone for them, and ultimately learn from them. "For someone who wasn't always great at friendship and was a lonely kid, I have been so lucky. I have such great friends."

Having a solid early friendship can set up expectations for your whole life. Tracy Moore is the host of popular Canadian daytime TV show *CityLine*. She met her first best friend in kindergarten. She can't remember who approached whom: "But I remember it happened quickly, and it was just this steadfast 'we're together' situation. We were in the same class every single year from kindergarten to grade eight." And although they came from different cultures—Andrea's family is German, and Tracy's is Jamaican—they fit right into each other's lives—two studious girls from close-knit families. "I was folded into her family from the get-go. I was there all the time. Andrea was at our house all the time. I went on trips with them. We were close!" They went to different high schools but stayed in touch. Without knowing the other's plan, they both applied and were accepted to McGill University, in Montreal. After they realized they'd both be in Montreal, they decided to room together: "A basement apartment with roaches on beautiful Avenue des Pins."

Now, as two married women with two kids each, they remain close friends. Tracy says, "I really do cherish that friendship. And it's not just about history, because I have had to move away from friendships where I had a lot of history. What's great about Andrea is that not only do we have a shared history, but we have a present connection, and that's important."

Having a friend who has known you forever can mean you are able to take bigger risks with each other. I sat down with Chriselle Lim, an old colleague who is the cofounder and chief marketing officer (CMO) of Bümo as well as a major lifestyle influencer. She's known her best friend for her whole life. That's because their mothers are best friends! Chriselle says,

> If you looked up the definition of a best friend, Lynette's photo would pop up because she just marks off all the checkpoints of what you expect a best friend to be. And I'm exactly the opposite. I am so career focused. I'm not saying people who are career focused can't be a good friend, but people who are so career focused and family driven, they kind of naturally forget about other things outside of your own world, unfortunately. Lynette has always pinpointed to me, like, "You're being a bad friend right now." She's always been super upfront. For instance, I'm the worst at birthdays. And every year, she knows that I won't remember her birthday. She will call me to remind me that it's her birthday in two weeks. And she blocked off that date for me, and I have to plan the entire day, and I cannot let my assistant do it for me.

Because of their long and close history together, Chriselle was able to take the criticism to heart and not get defensive. Lynette has helped her see that not tending to her friendships—not out of malice but out of her focus on work—comes with risks. "I've fucked up so much with friends, especially my best friend, but she is always *such* a good friend, being like, 'I forgive you, but you need to get better at this. I really think this could only happen with a childhood friend.'"

A 2019 study in *Childhood Development* found that the greatest predictor of romantic satisfaction in women was strong friendships with other girls in their teens. Through their friendships, girls learn assertiveness, social competence, intimacy, and stability. It makes sense; teenage romance is not known for longevity, let alone harmony, whereas friendships can last many years. Why wouldn't you be able to transfer your emotional knowledge from the friendship to the romantic ledger? Having repeated trouble with your current love life? Might be worth it to take a trip down memory lane and see if there is anything worth studying.

This isn't to say adolescent friendships are always rosy. In fact, they are often the most intense relationships of our lives. Degges-White explained to me, "When we're in the self definition period of our lives, we use our friends to define who we are." But much like our experience with siblings, even when our friendships were sometimes stormy as teenagers, that tension provided us much growth potential.

Unlike the time of my adolescence, tweens and teens today have to navigate the extra layer that tech adds to friendships. Not only are they together at school or in activities but also texts and social media have them in almost constant communication (or as much as their parents will allow). It's a lot of "togetherness" and not as much downtime to process the emotional ups and downs of this life stage. The physical distance of interacting online means young people are spending a lot of time in their relationships away from the body language and subtle cues of a face-to-face relationship. When you tease a friend by text, you don't see her face to make sure it landed as it was intended. There's almost no way to avoid misunderstandings online. Catherine Steiner-Adair, a clinical psychologist, says in *The Big Disconnect*: "As a species we are highly attuned to reading social cues. There's no question that kids are missing out on very critical social skills. In a way, texting and online communicating— it's not like it creates a nonverbal learning disability, but it puts everybody in a nonverbal disabled context where body language, facial expressions, and even the smallest kind of vocal reactions are rendered invisible." Yeah, the emojis are not cutting it.

I spoke to a friend's thirteen-year-old daughter about this aspect of teen friendships. Ella told me about how it goes down in her friend group: "There are certain girls who will act super-nice at school but then act not as nice to you on the internet." She's also acutely aware of how information can spread online. When I asked her how she'd deal with a rude remark or nasty joke online, she said, "I wouldn't want to go and tell a bunch of other people because I feel like that is how rumors start. They probably didn't realize that they were making a disrespectful or harmful joke, so I'd probably just go and talk to them directly."

Social media is known to encourage all of us to compare our lives to those of others in a way that creates anxiety and unhappiness. Steiner-Adair notes, "Girls are socialized more to compare themselves to other people, girls in particular, to develop their identities, so it makes them more vulnerable to the downsides to all of this." Ella recently noticed a lifelong friend falling into this trap:

She kind of always said inappropriate things you shouldn't say in general. And then this year at school she started saying that people at our school were not pretty and shouldn't post certain things on Instagram. I had another friend who noticed it too. And I decided that I really didn't want to be around someone who acted like that or had those ideas in her head or thought that kind of thing was okay, so I stopped hanging out with her as much. I didn't want to hurt her feelings, so I just slowly stopped hanging out with her. We're in different classes this year, so we already weren't hanging out as much.

It can also be telling to examine the friendship influences you had early in your life. Specifically, how did your parents model friendship for you? Like so many things, parents have great influence, for bad and good, in simply providing a role model for behavior. Were your parents really social, and did they go out a lot? Entertain a lot? Were they antisocial and avoidant? Did your mom have that one best friend, like the sister she never had? Did your dad have a tight crew? All of these things can have an impact on how you view your own friendships and role in them. So, it's important to take a look back to weed out the behavior that truly resonates with who you are now versus the behavior that colored you by proximity. Maybe you learned the value of entertaining or being the hostess with the mostest, and you've taken this into adulthood because you truly share your mom's passions, or maybe you don't, and you've forced yourself to be comfortable with certain types of socializing because that was programmed into you early, and you never thought to challenge it.

Even if it's not directly modeling friendship practices, your mom and dad's behavior might have had a big impact on the way you currently interact with your friends. My very good friend Sunny Hasselbring recalls how her mom dealt with conflict with the women in her family (Sunny is one of six sisters):

> My whole life, whenever my mom has had an issue with something that's going on with one of my sisters, she calls me, not my sister. So, it's something that I think I really learned growing up. And it's very female. My husband grew up one of three boys, and this *never* happens in their world. They just talk to each other so directly. It's so foreign to me. And I think as a result, I really did learn in my friendships to talk about friends with the other friends as an indirect way to try and resolve something, and when it comes to the big shit, that's never the right way to do it, never.

HOMEWORK:

Regardless of what stage you are at in your life right now, taking the time to examine some of your childhood patterns of friendship can provide valuable information on what motivates you in your current relationship and helps explain why you might be doing the things you do. Understanding what was planted in your subconscious through experience or the influence of family allows you to more consciously make choices about who you want to be and how you want to behave with the important people in your life. As a parent, it's worthwhile to consider how your friendships are a model for your child. What kind of friendships do you want for your kids? Know that these interactions not only affect you but also provide a blueprint for your child for years to come.

- Write down any memories of early significant friendships, for better or for worse. Can you see any of these behavior patterns cropping up in your current friendships?

- How did your parents or the influential adults in your life socialize? Are you similar or different? Can you see any behavior patterns cropping up in your current friendships?

"I have a need to make sure that we're collectively preserving what our heritage is, because when you grow up CBC, Canadian-born Chinese, like me, and the culture is so dominantly white—I don't want to lose that part of our collective community identity. Food is a big part of that. In Asian culture food is such a critical component of identity, we need to be able to go out with our friends for meals and eat the way we eat. You know, it's sloppy, it's loud by a Western standard, but for us it's normal. My Western friends might consider it quite rude, the sound we make when we eat, how we slurp. But it's definitely joyous when I'm with my Asian friends. Like, when we're getting together and eating food that Westerners might not love, it's amazing. It's like you have this little secret. *They're so dumb for not loving these chicken feet,* you know?"

LAINEY LUI
on the importance of the shared experience of
being Chinese with friends in Canada

CHAPTER 4

The Anatomy of a Good Friendship

Lots of people want to ride with you in the limo,
but what you want is someone who will ride the
bus with you when the limo breaks down.

Oprah Winfrey

I hear the word "toxic" thrown around a lot lately. "I need to get all of the toxic people out of my life." "She's toxic." "He's toxic." "She's such a bad friend." But if you're looking for true friendship that serves both of you, you need to understand that it's not about the other person or yourself. It's the relational quality between the two of you rather than a question of the other person being toxic. (I'm excluding outliers here who are overtly devilish. I'm talking about your normal run-of-the-mill friendships.) The reverse is also true, by the way. You'll hear people describe someone as being a "great friend" or themselves as a "good friend."

Neither of these extremes is true in a static way. A person with whom you've had conflict might be perfectly in sync with other people in her life. And that's because a friendship is a relationship *between* two people, and the *relationship* is toxic, bad, or great. The dynamic and the behavior that exist between two (or more) people create the relationship. So, in thinking about the anatomy of a great friendship, the first thing to do is stop talking about the other person in the relationship, or even yourself in the relationship, and focus on the dynamic between the two of you. What is working, and what isn't? If you find yourself listing why so-and-so is bad, you're missing the point. You have to understand *relationally* what's going on, and only then can you make a choice to fix it . . . or to walk away. This distinction between judging a person as a static entity and the relationship between two individuals is frequently misunderstood. I see the way confusion on this point has led to drama in my own life and all around me. After this concept clicks, you can start to take real ownership and responsibility for yourself and start to discover your own personal power. Or, as my dad says, "With 100 percent responsibility comes 100 percent freedom."

On the surface, there are obvious signs when a friendship is not working. But there are usually clues long before the obvious emerges, and this is where the self-awareness piece comes in. It's a feeling, a small anxiety, an angst that starts at a whisper but will get louder if you don't pay attention to it. In other words, it's not the *action* being taken but the way you are *feeling* in that relationship to which you need to be attuned. It can appear in small or big ways, depending on the situation. The more you lack self-awareness and either don't notice or ignore these feelings, the bigger they grow, to the great detriment of the relationship.

I spoke to Suzanne Degges-White, coauthor of *Forever Friends*, about what a bad friendship might look like, and she shared a simple answer: "You know yourself, and you don't like how you're behaving or how you feel in this relationship." This struck me because of the way she brought it back to self-knowledge: what feels good to you and what doesn't. What you will stand for and what you won't. When you're unaware of these things or consciously repressing some part of yourself to please others, it's easy to slip into these friendships that take far more than they give or to get complacent about longer-standing friendships that have started to become more of a bad habit than a purposeful choice.

This made me reflect back to when I went to college in Montreal. I had made friends with a really fun, interesting girl from Toronto. We quickly became close and hung out all the time, regularly hitting up bars and clubs all night and ditching class the following day. After about a year of this, I woke up one day and had had enough. I was behind on my work (my grade point average was terrible for the first time in my life), and I felt like crap. As I told my friend my plan to straighten up, I could see she was less than pleased. I tried to convince her to join me in dialing down the partying and was met with great resentment. Being new to college and new to the city, however, I was scared to really take a stand. And so I continued going out with her but with far less gusto. I kept bringing up my desire to make a change, and she kept resisting. But I just couldn't stand the way I felt—tired from going out and dealing with major anxiety from feeling pulled into situations I didn't want to be in. It wasn't who I was. I decided I had to cut ties with her completely, and when I did, I let out a big sigh of relief. Good for me. The problem was, however, that I simply deemed her a toxic friend and took no responsibility for the relationship. I had decided *she* was the problem. And I most certainly went around talking shit about her for the next several months to shine the light of responsibility away from myself. All these years later I can see that it was simply not true, and I let an opportunity to really grow slip right by. Sure, she had been the ringleader of our party circus, but I was most definitely an enthusiastic participant (at least for a time). What had I needed that she was offering? What about me was so magnetic for her? Upon reflection, she had many other friends, but I was the only one that would go out with her every night. Nobody was stopping me from staying home with my schoolwork. What we had between us didn't work. I wish I could have looked at what I found so compelling about that relationship and why I couldn't have navigated a shift in it rather than just cutting it off and laying all the blame at my old friend's feet. It would have helped me greatly along the way in my other relationships.

You might be thinking, *Well, I'm thirty-seven, and my clubbing days are over. This doesn't apply to me.* And it's true, this is a specific example with a clear problem attached to the relationship, but take away the details of my story, and this sort of behavior between friends happens all the time. How many times have you felt angst when you saw a friend's name on your call display but didn't address it? How many times have you become upset or frustrated about a repeated behavior from a friend but didn't say anything? How many times have you felt unseen or misunderstood by a friend and just swallowed it? Feel good? No. But yet we carry on, not feeling great. We're not listening to ourselves, don't have the confidence to act, or can't be bothered. In all cases, we end up compromising ourselves and our friendships.

No two people are the same, and it is infinitely less likely that any two friendships are the same. As such, there isn't a one-size-fits-all model for friendship. However, there are indisputable pillars of every good friendship—and in my opinion, they are non-negotiable for a healthy relationship that fortifies both partners. In fact, I will go one step further and say that if even one of these pillars is missing, the relationship will be more taxing on you. This is why it's paramount to understand those pillars and do a critical analysis of your current relationships. You need to know which relationships are working for you and which are falling short.

What does a good friendship look like? It's so much more than simply the people you happen to spend time with. Aristotle called these "accidental friendships" and noted that they are usually fleeting. He called those based on choice and mutual respect "friendships of good" and described them as evolving over a long time. Solid friendships require a combination of integrity, caring, and congeniality. But before you assess your friends, start by looking inward. In his book *How to Be a Friend*, Roman philosopher Cicero states that only moral people can have real friendships. By taking responsibility for our own behavior and prioritizing being a good friend, we increase the chances of having rich friendships. Being closely connected to a friend doesn't mean things are always breezy. A truly solid relationship can withstand tensions, disagreements, and even absences. Psychologists call this the *theory of rupture and repair*, and it is quintessential to any healthy relationship (we'll get into that in more detail later in this chapter).

Women get little training in conflict. In fact, most of us run from it. We keep our emotions bottled up and do anything not to rock the boat. Unfortunately, this keeps us numb. Over time, this numbing can lead to indifference toward others, making friendships less and less authentic. This inauthenticity undermines a friendship with a great basic structure because we'll avoid temporarily uncomfortable work and ultimately sabotage the relationship. And when I say "sabotage," I'm not talking about some big explosive ending—I'm talking about a subconscious acceptance of the mediocre as opposed to a conscious move toward the great.

Knowing what you should expect—both from yourself and from your friends—helps you know which relationships to focus on and which to move on from.

We've established that friendships are invaluable and that in order to attract good friends and be one yourself, you have to become your own best friend. But how do we recognize what a good friendship looks like? Do we accept the people who are simply around us most—coworkers, other students in a class, our partner's friends—as our de facto squad? Or do we swing the pendulum the other way and drop relationships at the first feeling of friction? Should a friend support you no matter what? Should friends be available whenever you want their company?

As I discussed in chapter 1, each friend brings out something different in us—obviously, they all bring their unique personalities to the table. There are also different ways to be friends—and we'll get into that more deeply in chapter 6. But when we're talking about good friendships, are there qualities we should look for and expect, and similarly, offer to friends ourselves? Yes, friends, there are. The following qualities must exist in a friendship for it to be great. If some are missing in a relationship, you might be in a new friendship or a less intimate one. But there are other elements no friendship can exist without.

Positivity

This seems obvious, right? We want to be around people that make us feel good. But being an analytical person, something about the word *positivity* grates on me. (Yikes! What does that say about me?) By nature, I'm a critical thinker. Also, a big part of my relationships is being able to vent about life's frustrations. Does that mean I'm doomed to be a bad friend?

I asked Shasta Nelson, author of *Frientimacy*, to clarify how she thinks about positivity within friendships. She explained that it's not about being sunshine and rainbows all the time, but in the context of friendship, positivity is anything that produces a good feeling. That can include listening, showing empathy, or giving compliments and praise. Laughter is one of the most powerful forms of positivity.

But what about my need for a good, old-fashioned bitch session? As I look back at my friendships, I realize I've spent time, *okay, a lot of time*, gabbing endlessly with my friends about old bosses, old boyfriends, current boyfriends, close female friends—the list goes on and on. What's worse is that I can't remember the exact details of each sesh, but I can totally remember how good they felt. Have I been a really bad friend all this time?

"This isn't about *being* positive," Nelson told me. "It's not to say you can't talk about negative things, and we can't whine. It's about making sure we all feel good at the end. It's a really important distinction. We don't want somebody walking away feeling judged or not accepted. So, positivity means making sure we enjoy each other and feel good around each other."

Phew. But what if I blow it? What if, unintentionally, I make a friend feel bad? In all relationships, a "magic ratio" must be maintained for us to feel good about them. "We know that we need to have five positive feelings for every negative feeling," says Nelson.

In terms of more obvious forms of positivity in friendships, you can't do much better than humor. And not just any humor—but the type that speaks to you and your friend. We've all had that experience of hanging with someone who is a nonstop joke machine, and we're exhausted by having to fake laugh all night. But when you spend time with someone with a shared sense of what is hilarious? It's a delicious bit of chemistry. Vivek Murthy explains in an article for Bluezones.com that laughter releases endorphins into our bodies, making us more relaxed. "Humor creates a powerful bond among people who all find the same thing funny. It's a form of common ground."

Friends who are authentically positive are absolute gems. Elise Loehnen describes one of her longest friendships in this way: "I have a tendency for overanalysis, and we all have that negativity bias, but she's good at saying 'Let's make it fun.' She's just unexpected and sort of delightful in a way that is very original. She just lets it be light in a way that's very refreshing for my soul. She doesn't let me stew. She's not denying my feelings, but she has a way of getting me up and out."

It's like the great Maya Angelou once said: "I've learned that people will forget what you said, people will forget what you did, but people will never forget how you made them feel."

Consistency

For friendships to thrive, you need to tend to them. If you don't make an effort to stay connected to friends, that connection weakens. And, as we learned during the quarantine, you don't have to be in the same room as your social group to be connected.

If you see a friend only once every six months, you're likely to spend your entire time together catching up on biographical details. How are the kids? Are you still at the same job? How was that trip you posted pictures of on Instagram? Is your partner still running triathlons? It's perfectly natural to want to share that kind of baseline information. If you don't see that friend for another six months, your next catchup is likely to go the same way. And that might be okay with both of you. But maybe what's really important to your friend in that moment is how she feels about her mother's health or that she feels lost in her career right now. Without more frequent and consistent time spent, you just don't have an opportunity to get below the surface. When you are seeing a friend more often, you don't need to spend all your time going over the basics—you both know where the other stands—and you can dive more deeply into what's actually important to you.

When I first met my relatively new friend Helene Corneau-Cohen at an event, we had almost immediate chemistry. We were both Canadian, we both loved fashion, and we found out after the fact that we live only one block apart. In Los Angeles, that's really something. Upon getting to know Helene, who has moved a lot in her adult life, I know that making and keeping new connections is really important to her. When I asked her what she thought the secrets to maintaining a good friendship were, she replied,

> I think maybe openness—you can be open in a different way in friendship because your obligation to that person is different (in friendship) compared to a romantic relationship. There is a weight from responsibility of a committed romantic relationship—that comes with a husband and family—that you don't have in friendship, that allows a certain freedom that exists in a platonic relationship—in that freedom, you can access a different part of yourself through the friendship relationship. Maybe you can be more vulnerable because there is less immediacy of stress or responsibility. But the flip side of that is that because there is less responsibility, people in friendships can grow complacent. Commitment, or lack thereof, really is the plague of today's friendships. A truly great friendship will strike the balance of freedom and commitment.

Vulnerability

This is one of the hardest and most important parts of friendship and something I struggle with regularly. For most of my relationships, I play the role of "the rock."

I'm the one friends can count on in a time of need. If they need important life advice on something serious and time sensitive, I'm their gal. And I take a lot of pride in that role. But along with that comes a lot of walls. If I'm the fixer, then how can I show any "weakness"? Won't that ruin my friendship brand? But the truth is, I don't really have a friendship brand if I'm not showing my true colors. And I want to be clear, of course I've had emotional moments with my friends when the shit has really hit the fan (a death, a breakup—I mean, I'm not a robot!), but that's not what I'm talking about. I'm talking about sharing those smaller, more nuanced fears and insecurities about who you are, what path you're on, and which choices you're making.

The process of becoming close to someone is to see and be seen. No amount of time spent together can overcome a lack of vulnerability. Facing your fear about your fears is simply one of the most powerful things you can do both for yourself and for your friends.

We're all a ridiculous mashup of charm, jealousy, compassion, and bad moods (at least). If you know someone who never lets her guard down, who never admits to mistakes or screwups, who will not express weakness—that person is not your friend. You might like her, but you can't be close with this sort of person. And the same is true on your part.

We feel better when we know our friends understand—or likely share—our shortcomings. When another mom tells me she feels like trash because she snapped at her kid, I'm able to empathize because I've been there, and because I know she's a good person, I also feel better about myself. *There's connection there.*

It takes courage to put yourself out there emotionally, which isn't to say that everyone deserves a front-row seat to your emotional life. Be sure that the friends you share most with have earned that right.

Trust

In order to allow ourselves to be vulnerable with a friend, we have to establish trust. If you're going to ask a friend to help deconstruct the sexual dry spell you and your boyfriend are going through, you need to feel confident that she won't share it with the rest of your friend group. And you shouldn't need to say, "Please don't repeat this." A good friend should have the sense to know what you wouldn't want out in the world.

You can gauge how trustworthy a friend is by paying attention to how she talks about other people. Do you get the most juice about mutual friends from her? If so, assume they're getting the same about you.

We can build up our own trustworthiness by being good listeners, expressing sympathy and support for friends' challenges, and noting their successes—basically receiving them in a caring way.

Building trust isn't only about discretion but about actions. A good friend should be someone you can count on—to be there for you, to do what she says she's going to do, and most importantly to have your best interests at heart. This doesn't mean that friends have to be on call at all times, but it's reasonable to expect that a good friend has your back.

Balance

A good friendship requires balance. Meaning, we need to be in the *same friendship*. If I have to text you four times for each response I get from you, we're out of sync. If my friend calls me once a week to meet for coffee, and I have the inclination to see her only once a month, she's going to feel like I'm avoiding her. In *Answers for Aristotle,* Massimo Pigliucci writes, "It makes perfect sense that you could be in love with someone who doesn't reciprocate your feelings, but it is incoherent to say that one has a non-reciprocal friendship." This is one of the most challenging areas within female friendships. In a romantic relationship, you likely couldn't get beyond five dates before you started to outline the expectations you have of each other. In sexual relationships, the question is normally, "Are you seeing other people?" Obviously, that's not a question in friendships. But finding a frequency and an intensity that feels right to both people in a friendship is important to the satisfaction they both get from it. And without that balance, it's easy for someone to feel rejected or smothered.

My friend Anne told me about an imbalanced friendship she had and how she only saw that for what it was after the fact. She and her Pilates instructor would hang around after class and talk, sometimes for hours. The conversations were both lively and intimate. Anne loaned her teacher clothes for events (including Anne's own wedding dress), she invited her teacher to the theater when she had an extra ticket, and they would exchange shine on Instagram. This went on for years. As many are, the Pilates studio was expensive, and Anne eventually decided that it was more financially responsible to start working out at home, so she stopped taking classes. And then Anne saw the teacher's wedding on Instagram, and it felt like a gut punch. "I said to my husband, 'Oh, so we weren't really friends.' And he just looked at me and said, 'Uh, *yeah*. She was your Pilates teacher,' like it was so obvious. I was hurt, to be honest, but I wasn't mad. I just realized that I had it twisted. She liked me, but we weren't the close friends I thought we were. We were in two very different friendships."

Maybe friendships should come with contracts. My friend Jette Miller thinks so. She doesn't literally mean you should deliver paperwork to someone you've recently clicked with. But she does believe in finding ways to communicate how a friendship exists in her life. "If you meet someone, and you really click, and you think they want a close relationship with you, I think a great conversation would be, 'Oh, I wish I was living on the other side of town because I have my friends here that I see every day, but it's cool that we can see each other once a week.'" I really like this idea of letting a friend know—in loving terms, of course—what you've got the capacity for at that moment.

Boundaries

In her book *Rising Strong*, Brené Brown defines boundaries simply as what's okay and what's not okay. Being able to set boundaries for ourselves is not something we're taught—particularly as women—in this culture. Women are raised to accommodate, make nice, and make everyone comfortable—none of which stops us from noticing when people do things we don't like. But that cultural practice of swallowing any negative emotion can make us resentful. Brown goes on to say that a mindset shift in which you assume everyone is doing their best can release you from those resentments. But even with this spirit of generosity, you still have to be willing to set and maintain boundaries.

People will have their own boundaries, depending on what they care about. But some common boundaries many people care about frequently get trespassed.

Time: What feels less abundant than time these days? We're all scrambling from task to task, trying to make our way through impossible to-do lists. So, it's more than just annoying when a friend is chronically late. Everyone hits a snag sometimes, but a friend who is always fifteen or twenty minutes late is letting you know what she thinks of your time.

Values: It's great to have friends from different backgrounds and beliefs—it helps us build empathy and grow as humans. But if your values aren't being respected, you need to rethink the relationship. Notice I didn't say *share* your values. There's a big difference. Maybe you're not a believer, and one of your friends is a weekly churchgoer. If she makes repeated invitations for you to attend with her, you'd have to consider how much she respects your point of view. Likewise, if you can't respect someone's values—they vote for someone you find reprehensible—you're not going to be able to be close.

You (and They) Can Be Honest

We want our friends to be our fans. It feels amazing to be around people who laugh at our jokes, find our observations fascinating, and generally find our company delightful. What it doesn't mean is that friends need to be "yes" women. Between close friends, there should be enough trust for there to be honesty.

Honesty between friends doesn't mean a constant outpouring of opinions. A friend who's got something to say about every move you make might deserve a demotion. But if a friend asks you for your thoughts about her plan to move to Montreal to live with a guy she met last month online, you should feel comfortable enough to be straight with her. Of course, you need to tell her what a terrible idea it is in the kindest, warmest way you can. It's actually not that hard to tell friends their plans are bonkers without saying it at all. You can ask questions, such as, "How do you think it will feel to be in a city where you only know him?" Or, "Are you able to work there?" Or, "Do you have a plan for what to do if the relationship doesn't work out?"

Likewise, if you go to a friend for her counsel, you need to be prepared to hear what she really thinks—not just what you want to hear. Jette handles both scenarios in a way I really admire. She makes it clear when she wants feedback by saying to friends, "Be straight with me," or, "I really want your feedback." So, she lets friends know that it's safe to be honest. She manages her own desire to be honest with friends by asking explicitly, "Do you want my advice?" rather than simply sounding off.

I asked Anna Cho, a child psychologist, about this. She told me, "I think when you're empowered with your own voice and you have trials, you can challenge yourself to speak up in small, repetitive ways. Then you're not off-loading all at once. Some people are better at those smaller exchanges, whereas some people are more emotionally extreme. I think what fuses it all is self-awareness."

I have had the good fortune to have had many healthy, platonic relationships with men in my life and have noticed a decided difference in male friendships. In my experience, they have fewer but longer friendships over the course of a lifetime. Almost all of my brother's friends, as well as my male friends, are still deeply connected to the friends from their youth (with very few spots on the bench for newcomers). Degges-White has made a similar observation about her own son. "He's as close to his high school and college buddies, to his middle school buddies, as anyone I've ever met. He's been a best man at three weddings!"

It's so easy to become siloed in our relationships—with all our friends a lot like us politically, professionally, emotionally—and as a result we risk losing the ability to tolerate small frictions. Cho told me, "If a person is just mirroring you, then there's nothing new happening. Unless there is some turbulence, there's not much life in that." We have to be willing to allow for some turbulence, through honesty, if we want friendships that really live.

There is a simplicity to these friendships, something quite beautiful, really. Guys know what to expect; they feel totally comfortable. It's almost as if they speak a secret language. While I wouldn't trade in my ride-or-dies for anything in the world—nuance, complexity, drama, and all—there is most definitely something worth noting from these male friendships. Their honesty. Their clarity of voice. Specifically, between my brother and his friends, and between my male friends, I've witnessed that the way they deal with conflict or challenge in relationships is simple, direct, and effective. If there is a problem, they address it. Not with a ton of words, no great pomp or circumstance. Not with great angst. It seems to go something like this:

This is the problem. This is how I feel about it. What do we do about it?

That's it.

Even when I look at my own interactions with my male friends, the dialogue around conflict seems a lot more open and straightforward. Usually if I have a problem with one of my male friends, I don't think twice about calling them out. And yet with my female friends . . . well, it's complicated. Why is that?

I asked Cho about why this might be happening. She responded,

> I think boys are more immediate and explicitly connected through physical activities. They are connected to and grounded through their bodies. They learn through the rules of the game. The girls have more minimal exposure to physical expression, to their bodies. They might find their voice through dressing up or role playing but not by getting into their bodies as much. And I think that something happens when young kids do get into their bodies. When you're in your body from a young age, there is a concrete connection to what you want and need.

While I am reluctant to assign strict gender roles to anything, as the world becomes more fluid, it is certainly interesting to think about that strong connection to the body that boys seem to have (or have been socialized to have) at such a young age and how that connection might influence their communication style in relationships.

Rupture and Repair

For me this is one of the most important concepts in friendship—and one many women run from. *Rupture and repair* is a classic psychotherapy term, as described by therapist Karen Koenig:

> Rupture and repair is an often-used clinical phrase, which applies to a breach in the therapeutic relationship followed by its restoration and positive continuation. A rupture may be caused by an overt disagreement between therapist and client, a client holding on to negative feelings about something a therapist said or did or didn't say or didn't do, or any disturbance in their cordial equilibrium. This dynamic is not something that client and therapist need to avoid. In fact, it's something they should both welcome as proof of the strength of their connection and bond.

This idea rings equally true in friendship. If you have a long standing relationship of any consequence with someone, conflict will arise. This is a fact. You simply can't go through life with someone and not face adversity at some point—not if it's a real relationship. But the sad truth is that many, including me, have avoided dealing with things to keep things copacetic. This move, however, shortchanges everyone involved. By not dealing with things as they come up, you mute your own voice and stifle the relationship. By dealing with conflict—the rupture—and working on the repair, you show respect to yourself, the other, and the relationship, a move that facilitates growth and love.

Anita Chakrabarti, a psychiatrist I know well, thinks a lot about the parts of a relationship that make it healthy. She says,

> The rough edge *between* people is where the spark is. There is always turbulence in a relationship, and

that turbulence gives both friends a chance to grow emotionally. That is one of the most important things about friendships—you get to learn about how someone else sees the world and realize that they see it differently than you do. If the relationship has trust and affection, the hostility that inevitably comes up between two people is contained, so the aggression is overcome, and the friends work together to grow and learn something new. Having friends that are a lot like you decreases the amount that you can learn from the other person. So, it is okay to have friends that mirror you, being like you; but if you want to grow and learn, it is good to have friends that are different. So, transformation and growth involve turbulence, difference, and a lot of learning; all the while keeping a connection healthy. These are the things that make a friendship special and important.

Letting problems fester without addressing them—either you're passive and downplay your own feelings or are just wholly unaware of what's going on for you—can really do a number on your relationship. This type of behavior marginalizes your own feelings and thoughts and manifests in latent feelings of irritation or frustration with the relationship. This often results in passive-aggressive behavior—not saying what's on your mind but acting aloof or annoyed. Again, not great for the relationship. It does not allow you to get your feelings out or for your friend to understand what's going wrong. And finally, because we aren't used to saying what's on our minds, when we do confront a situation, we can overdo it and have a bigger-than-necessary reaction. You might come off as heated and aggressive, but really you're just nervous. After we're aware of our own feelings, we need to learn how to communicate them honestly—as opposed to reactively—in a timely manner.

As I reflected on the state of my own relationships, I realized I've avoided rupture and repair *a lot*. I wanted to start correcting it, and when I thought of specific circumstances I might address, I couldn't believe how much apprehension I had. *What is it about just saying how we feel?* I decided I was going to do something about it and set out to speak to a friend who was constantly late. Like, *late* late. Not once in a blue moon but chronically. And it irked me every time. In fact, it had been getting so irritating to me that I would need to spend the first half hour with her just internally calming myself down. I had resorted to passive comments or jokes over her tardiness in the past, but unsurprisingly, to no great effect. This time, however, I would address it head on. As I went to meet her, it was amazing what my mind was doing. From the time I turned on the ignition until I handed my keys to the valet, I was trying to minimize her being late (and marginalize my own feelings). *Was it really necessary to create something out of nothing?* I kept saying to myself. But it wasn't nothing. It was really getting in the way of our friendship, and I had to say something. And nothing told me that more than when I arrived and of course . . . she arrived thirty minutes after I did.

I couldn't believe how nervous I was. I feel kind of pathetic even writing this out for all to see. But I was really nervous. Like what was the worst thing that could happen? This is the problem with not being upfront in the first place, however. A reasonably small irritation can turn into an explosion if you avoid it, and that's what it felt like was about to happen. As the minutes clicked by, I had played out every scenario and felt myself getting angrier as I thought about all the time I had wasted—and then she walked in. As I waved hello, I decided I just had to own my inner dude (or *animus*, for all of you psychology geeks out there), and say what was on my mind. I reminded myself:

This is the problem. This is how I feel about it. What do we do about it?

This is the problem. This is how I feel about it. What do we do about it?

This is the problem. This is how I feel about it. What do we do about it?

So, with little small talk, I just started in on it. "I want to talk to you about something . . ." I was immediately met with the "story" of what had happened: traffic, jerk boss, and so forth. It would have been easy to take the out she was giving me. But this time I didn't.

I have to admit, it was tough. At first, after it was clear I wasn't accepting excuses this time, things weren't all that warm and fuzzy. There was a lot of defensiveness: "You're not being understanding." It wasn't until I stopped talking about the details ("You were thirty minutes late for dinner at Chaya." "You're exaggerating! I was only ten minutes late; I told you the valet had disappeared!") and started talking about how I was feeling, what it represented to me, and how it was affecting our friendship that things started to take a turn. It was only then that we could get into the meat of what was really going on. What was interesting is that after I had a chance to say my piece, she let me in on a couple of things I had done that had bothered her (not as a tit for tat but as a genuine feeling), and we were able to clear the air.

All and all, I'd say we both left that meeting exhausted but with a renewed sense of hope for our relationship and a clear love for one another. And, I think, one of my biggest takeaways was that the fear that had built up prior to talking to her was completely unjustified. After I had ripped off the Band-Aid, I felt comfortable saying what I felt, and I think I still would have even if things started to go badly. There really is power to saying how you feel.

I love the way Ralph Waldo Emerson describes this need for healthy friction (yes, he says "manly," but this was more than a hundred years ago!):

> Friendship requires that rare mean betwixt likeness
> and unlikeness, that piques each with the presence
> of power and of consent in the other party . . . I
> hate, where I looked for a manly furtherance, or at
> least a manly resistance, to find a mush of concession.
> Better be a nettle in the side of your friend, than his
> echo. The condition which high friendship demands
> is ability to do without it . . . Let it be an alliance
> of two large formidable natures, mutually beheld,
> mutually feared, before yet they recognize the deep
> identity which beneath these disparities unites them.

It Happens over Time

One of the things I have noticed almost without exception in my relationships (both friendships and romances) is the quicker they start, the quicker they end. A mistake many people make is to meet someone; feel that wonderful click of meeting a like-minded person; and then proceed to over-share, over-request, and basically overdo. No matter how deep into a friend crush you are, you have to be cognizant of how long and how well you truly know this person. It takes time to get to know someone and to reveal ourselves.

Jeffrey Hall, a professor of communication studies at the University of Kansas, looks at friendships and how they develop. In a 2018 study, Hall asked participants to record how close they felt to new friends over time. He discovered that to go from meeting a person to becoming a casual friend takes between 40 and 60 hours, to transition from casual friends to friends takes between 80 and 100 hours, and to reach the pinnacle of best friendship takes about 200 hours.

When you think about how much time you have each week to invest in your friendships, it really brings those numbers to life. Let's say you see a new friend for an hour or two every two weeks. According to Hall's research, you wouldn't even be solid friends at about ten months!

Of course, how you spend time with someone dictates how close you can become. You might have spent hundreds of hours next to a coworker, but if your conversations are only ever courteous, "Hey, how was your weekend?" and never go deeper, you aren't going to feel like close friends.

In an interview with Oprah Winfrey, Brown urges people, "Share with people who have earned the right to hear your story." Nelson notes that when people learn about the importance of vulnerability, it's easy for them to forget the level of intimacy they have with their friends. "They meet near strangers and think we should just tell each other everything, and then we'll be close. No. You can't do vulnerability without consistency and positivity. It has to be vulnerability that feels safe and appropriate for that relationship and where you feel good having shared it as opposed to having a vulnerability hangover."

HOMEWORK

The characteristics fundamental to a strong and lasting friendship are not only good for forging relationships but also great traits to have as an individual in general. Having awareness about and working on your own positivity, trustworthiness, vulnerability, and consistency not only ensures that you can pull your weight in relationships but also creates the confidence to demand the same.

- Think of your most important friendships. Make a list. For each, write down which of the following are being met and which aren't: trust, consistency, honesty, reciprocity, boundaries.

- Make a list of your boundaries. If you think you don't need any, just think about what grates on you, even with friends you really love. That's almost always a sign that you need a boundary around that feeling.

- List the past two to three times you've been irritated by someone's behavior and haven't spoken up. Why didn't you tell your friend about what was bothering you? Have you ever brought a problem to a friend? How did it go?

- Make a list of the people who consistently cross your boundaries. Now ask yourself, have you communicated clear boundaries, or are they simply living in your head?

- Make a list of three to five times when, upon reflection, you think you might have crossed a friend's boundaries. How was it handled?

- Practice calmly letting friends know what bothers you. If you are feeling uneasy, start with the smaller stuff and work your way up to the things that have the potential for bigger conflict.

"**M**any years ago, one of my friends introduced me to a CD by Dr. Marsha Linehan called *From Suffering to Freedom Through Acceptance*. She said, 'Anita, you've got to listen to this, you are going to love it. Let's sit down and listen right now.' We sat down, I can remember exactly where we were and how deeply the exercises resonated with me. I could immediately see how they would help me with the work that I was doing with patients. My friend knew intuitively that I would really appreciate the exercises. She understood both me, my values, and my work. I resisted at first, but she seemed to know how important it would be for me before even I knew it. I still use those exercises in my work and have used them regularly for the past twenty years with patients, in groups, and with all kinds of people. It was a significant turning point in knowledge and technique in my career. But that shared moment is also a part of our friendship. Each time I listen to the exercises I think of my friend and her understanding, generosity, and insistence that I really listen.

My friend and I talk often, and many times our points of view are very different. We both have lots of ideas, and I find myself thinking again: 'What on earth is she talking about? That sounds like nonsense.' But then I remember her insistence I listen to the Linehan exercises, and I think to myself, 'No, slow down. Wait a minute. I have a trust in her,' and even if it sounds like her idea is from another planet, I give what she is saying serious consideration because in that experience that we shared as friends, I learned that in our differences we have much to teach each other."

ANITA CHAKRABARTI
on how absolute trust deepens friendship

CHAPTER 5

When More Is So Much Less

Perfection is achieved not when there is nothing more to add but when there is nothing left to take away.

ANTOINE DE SAINT-EXUPÉRY

I am always amazed when I talk to my female friends or colleagues who have half a dozen "friend events" each week — baby shower on Sunday, after-work drinks on Thursday, mani-pedi meet-up on Monday. Forever caught in the vortex of buying gifts or saving the dates. Frankly, it's exhausting for me just to listen to it. Does that make me a shitty friend? Why don't I want to do all this stuff?

A lightbulb went on for me as I began to do my preliminary research for this book. In *How to Get Sh*t Done*, I describe how we think of busyness as a modern form of bragging, when really it is a sexy cover for fear-based overscheduling (i.e., not wanting to be alone, even for a second, with our thoughts). There's a similar modern misunderstanding that having an endless roster of friends proves our worth. Having a lot of "friends" makes us feel popular, allows us to avoid ourselves, and helps us avoid the intimacy required for real relationships. Not so great.

This realization was one of the driving forces for me in writing this book. When friendships don't live up to what we now know they should be, it's time to act. There is no way you can accommodate more than a handful of people as true friends. Friendships that are worthwhile take time, work, effort, and energy in a way that wouldn't be possible with dozens of friends. It's simple math. Unfortunately, social media has pushed this friendship math from basic arithmetic to algebra.

Outside personal relationships, we've started embracing minimalism. We're sparking joy with our material possessions (thanks, Marie) and quieting our noisy world (we hear you, Cal). Oddly, this idea of minimalism hasn't been applied to the most important aspect of our lives: *our relationships*. Less really is more, and our friendships are no exception. We just need to put some structure around how to do that.

Cultural critic Maria Popova remarked, "We are living in a time where the very word 'friend' has become completely diluted and almost meaningless—think, counting the number of people who follow you on Facebook and listed as 'friends.'" The average person has more than three hundred friends on Facebook. Yikes! But let's be honest, many of those are a trail mix of summer camp friends, cousins you haven't seen in five years, and people you worked with three jobs ago. We call peers we barely know "friends," we call all colleagues "friends," we mistake mutual admiration for friendship, and we name-drop acquaintances as "friends" for personal gain. Don't get me wrong. It's nice to be friendly. It makes the world better. It makes us better. But I agree with Popova that we're diluting the meaning of the word. Ralph Waldo Emerson wrote extensively on the value of friendships and felt strongly about this too: "I hate the prostitution of the name friendship to signify modish and worldly alliances."

Emerson believed in a robust definition of friendship. He wrote that friendship

> is for aid and comfort through all the relations
> and passages of life and death. It is fit for serene
> days, and graceful gifts, and country rambles, but
> also for rough roads and hard fare, shipwreck,
> poverty, and persecution. . . . We are to dignify
> to each other the daily needs and offices of man's
> life, and embellish it by courage, wisdom and
> unity. It should never fall into something usual
> and settled, but should be alert and inventive, and
> add rhyme and reason to what was drudgery.

I don't know about you, but I don't want to live through a shipwreck with my cousin's hairdresser, whom I met at her wedding.

By referring to acquaintances and best friends by the same title, we're corroding our sense of what friendships are. We also put ourselves in tricky situations in which we don't know how much time and emotional energy we should be putting into all our "friends." What if we returned to an Aristotelian proposal that the highest form of friendship is one of virtue? Embedded in Aristotle's description of friendship is growth; its very purpose is to help you evolve.

So, how do we resolve this conundrum? Friendship has been co-opted by social media. We know these networks are friendly rather than made up of real friends. I propose a more accurate description of these different kinds of relationships. By specifying "work friends," "school friends," and "dog park friends," we can leave the label of friend for those we're truly connected with.

If we're looking to improve our lives by improving our friendships, it's worthwhile to look at how many you can actually invest in. We know that friendships require our attention, or they become stale. What's a realistic number of friends?

Robin Dunbar, an evolutionary biologist from the University of Oxford, has studied just that. He began his work with chimpanzees, looking at how their brain size related to the size of their social groups. He then looked at various human societies—from hunter-gatherer tribes to army units—to see how human brain size relates to our social circles. He concluded that our cognitive limit for friends is about 150 people. That's your posse. Or rather, you really can't handle more than that, cognitively. The number of people you'd consider good friends is lower, naturally, at 50 people. The next level consists of the people you'd turn to with a secret or a problem, and there are about 15 of those. And at the pinnacle, your closest friends constitute a group of about 5.

Social media have allowed us to connect with far more people than we otherwise would or could. And it's a great way to keep a pulse on family members or childhood friends who live far away. You can hit "like" on the photo of your friend's newborn. You can leave a crying-laughing emoji on her rant about her husband. You can send a birthday wish to your second-grade teacher. But there are ways digital connection cannot mimic in-person time with friends. You lose out on the real-time experience of an event together, sometimes in subtle ways. For example, you're having coffee with a friend, and she realizes you caught her eyeing the waiter, and you both crack up. Or you tear up when she's crying over a loss. The other experience you can't replace with your laptop is physical. When a friend gives us a hug, touches our shoulder to emphasize a point, pats our back, it communicates affection, and it triggers a flood of endorphins.

Anthropologists believe the endorphin rush primates receive when grooming each other encourages belonging to a group, which improves their chance of survival. With what we know about the dangers of loneliness, it makes sense that our own evolution requires us to feel good when we're close to those we care about. Wasn't one of the most bittersweet parts of quarantine seeing friends give long-distanced, pantomime "hugs"? And maybe the worst thing social media does is create the sense that other people have more friends or are having more fun with friends than we are.

In his research, Tim Kasser identified two values that influence how our relationships affect our well-being: (1) popularity, the drive to be liked by many people, and (2) affinity, the drive to build close, strong relationships. Kasser found that people driven by popularity were less happy and more depressed than those driven by affinity. Social media encourages popularity-driven behavior in many ways—most obviously in the way it frames experiences with thumbs-up and sad-face emojis and hearts and likes.

My friend and colleague Jette Miller admits to being up in her feelings about this.

> I hear about other friends of mine going out, and I get FOMO because they're hanging out with all these people. And doing stuff with all these people. I literally have a pang, a physical reaction of longing to be part of whatever is going on at that moment. Sometimes, it's almost jealousy. Recently, I've had to stop myself and think, "What's wrong with me?" Realistically, I can't have all these friendships and all these connections. That realization comes with this sense of loneliness, but the number one question I have to keep asking myself is how do I want to be in a relationship, and what's my capacity? How many friends can I have and have a satisfying connection with them? Probably not so many.

The other major constraint on how many friends we can have is time. We know that intimacy requires us to spend hours with people. A study in the *Journal of Personal and Social Relationships* shows that it takes about 200 hours to become close friends with someone (obviously, other elements have to be in play also, such as vulnerability). Maintaining that closeness also takes time. Dunbar says you need to interact with your inner circle of friends once a week in order to stay close. Given that feeling pressed for time is perhaps *the* shared experience of our era, it's worth thinking carefully about how your friendships are affected by your schedule. You only have so much time and energy, and whether you're spending it online or in real life, that amount isn't much changed. So, while you can feel like you're connected to many more people via social media, you're still really only able to do justice to that same small number of friendships. Of course, some people are naturally more social than others and can manage a larger friend group. But for most of us, more friends simply mean we're spreading ourselves thinner, like some kind of shameless "friend slut." (Okay, I know that sounds a little gross, but I'm telling you, it came up in more than a few interviews.)

An article in *Personal and Social Psychology Review* examined what we get from close relationships and found that people look to their closest friends to do two things: offer strong support and act as a relational catalyst; in other words, people who help you through hard times and celebrate with you in great times. Without undermining the value of acquaintances, you likely wouldn't turn to them when looking for either of those experiences.

Tracy Moore, host of *CityLine*, has a lot of friends. Working on a popular morning show means she's interacting with a lot of people each day—from crew to regular guests to audience members and, of course, her family.

"There are workplace friends, guest expert friends. There's my gym family. And I've been vulnerable with all of these people. But there is an openness that only happens with the core." Her "core" is made up of three other women she's known since college, and those are the friends with whom she feels she can be her truest self. "I don't spread myself around because I have to be stingy with my energy, or there would be nothing left for my family. I've had friends like that who let everyone in. And you know what? As a friend, I felt cheated. Like, you let everyone in, you're available for everyone? Who is special?"

You might think someone who created an app to connect mothers in need of mom friends would be all about a big friend circle. But Michelle Kennedy, the entrepreneur behind Peanut, is absolutely not. If your friends aren't having kids at the same time you are, motherhood can be really lonely. Then there's the minefield of parenting style. Peanut allows women to connect with like-minded moms in their area. Those relationships can be life-, or at least sanity-, saving. However, Kennedy believes it's important to be judicious when you're onboarding friends.

> I think the analysis piece is important, and I don't think people do that. I think they dial it in and go through the motions. They operate out of guilt. I know a lot of mom friends that are still trying to maintain thirty friends, and that's just preposterous, right? So that actually, to me, *is the definition of not a good friend*. You can't possibly be fulfilling the needs or the responsibilities of what a true friendship is if you've got a newborn and thirty friends, or a toddler and thirty friends. The math doesn't add up.

A new friend of mine, Helene Corneau-Cohen, expressed it in a different way:

I just don't like it when someone calls everyone their "friend." Like that word is precious to me. I was sitting at dinner the other night with a really good friend of mine, and another woman approached the table to say hi. My friend jumped up and quickly introduced me, "Helene, I want you to meet my great friend Susan!" *Your great friend Susan?* I thought to myself. I've known you fifteen years, never once heard of Susan! When my friend sat back down, I asked how she knew her great friend Susan, to which she nonchalantly replied, "We worked together last year on a job." I can't say exactly why, but it really bothered me. It's like, you're diluting what friendship really is if you so easily slap that label on everyone you've ever met!

This made me stop and think. Looking at my own behavior, I most definitely have introduced people as friends who were really only acquaintances or colleagues. In my defense, I consciously made that choice because I wanted there to be a sense of warmth and comfort; I wanted them to feel important to me in some way. But maybe my good intentions aren't necessary if they don't really reflect the truth of the situation? Further, I needed to look not only at what I thought I was doing for the other person but also at what presenting people as closer to me than they were was actually doing for *me and my psyche.*

The value of a small, core group of friends only increases as we age. A study by social psychologist Bill Chopik of Michigan State University found that friendships do more for our health and well-being as we get older. But quality counts. He says, "Having closer friends is better than having many superficial friends."

Sasha Tong cohosts with Lainey Lui the podcast *What's Your Drama,* which gives advice to people who write in with their dilemmas. It's insightful, hilarious, and full of swearing. Many of the questions are about problems in friendships. Both hosts have what they call "stranger danger":

> The danger was probably born out of me being quite shy and introverted. And I think it did start out as a protective measure. Like, *Who are these people? Do I want to let them in?* I've always had such a tight group of friends, I think of myself as a ride-or-die. And I think as I've gotten older, I realized that I can only really be of good value to so many people without dropping the ball. I only have a limited capacity when it comes to actually being a good friend. So, I'm very, very picky about who I invite into my life. So, for me, that is what stranger danger is.

Tong's best-friend group, which includes Lui, is made up of six women. Although they sometimes split off into smaller groups, they prefer the energy that's created when they're all together, whether in backyard pandemic hangs or in text threads. But her best friend, Emily, lives out West:

> She's always been my friend, but we were never tight until high school grade eight. She is just one of those magic friends, you know, where everything's aligned, like the way we think about things. We had similar fathers and these heroic mothers. We love our moms and our sisters in ways that seem very abnormal to other people, but we find it very normal. The trust is unbreakable. I don't trust anybody more than I do her. Like, if I only had her, I'd still be fulfilled.

Lauren Gallo, a marketing executive, told me, "I have a group of girlfriends called 'the bunnies.' Ever since I was a kid, I used to call my dearest friends bunnies. I always felt it was endearing. We are all the ultimate support group for each other. Each of us is very different but brings great perspective, warmth, support, laughs, and advice."

HOMEWORK

It's not that I'm discouraging you from having lots of friends—only encouraging you to get realistic about how many friends you can really engage with in a deep way. By being deliberate about who you spend the most time with consistently, you can develop better friendship practices, give more to your friendships, and get more out of them too. After you're being purposeful about who you want to spend time with—and who you don't want to spend time with—it's likely that the number of people you consider close friends will naturally contract. When you know yourself and the kind of energy you want around you, it becomes increasingly obvious which friendships it makes sense to invest in.

- Think about the people you consider your close friends. How much time do you spend with them each month? Is it enough? If it's not, what's keeping you apart?

- How much time do you spend on social media each week? (Check your phone for an accurate number.) How does your answer to this question compare with your answer to the previous one?

"I just got married, and I couldn't find a dress for the Jewish wedding because I needed it to be conservative, a certain length. It was literally the lockdown, quarantine, so no stores were open, and I had to order it online. I kept ordering things and returning them because nothing worked. One of my longtime friends comes to dinner with her new husband.

I had texted one of my longtime friends about how frustrated I was about not finding a dress, and she wrote back right away, 'I have the perfect dress for you. You'll have to go get it tailored. I'll bring it tomorrow. You can totally have it if it works.'

Well, it was beautiful. 'I can get it tailored?' I asked. She's like, 'You can have it. It's yours!'

I was beyond thrilled. The dress was beautiful, so I went to the tailor the next day, and they could easily adjust it. I was so happy. I texted her to thank her and tell her the dress would work perfectly.

But then a few hours later, I got a text back saying, 'So, let's talk money. How much are you going to pay me for it?'

I was confused. I definitely didn't remember her saying I had to pay for it. I scrolled all though my phone, and she said I could have it since it hadn't fit.

The dress turned out to be worth $1,700, which I totally couldn't afford. I felt frustrated because my friend is financially doing okay and knows that I'm not necessarily in the same position as her. I didn't want her to think I just assumed I wouldn't pay for the dress, even though she didn't make it clear that was her intention. So I offered to pay $400 for it because the tailoring would cost another $100.

The anxiety that I had for those two hours was insane because I was just like, *'I want the dress!* I don't want to keep looking. I already have it.' The anxiety was killing me.

She wrote me back, 'I was thinking closer to $750 because I can get that on The RealReal.' I started to get really bothered. Why hadn't she brought this up in the beginning? I also started thinking about all of the money I laid out for her wedding. She had lavish engagement parties, no expenses spared events. Why couldn't she just have given me the dress out of the kindness of her heart?

She wound up writing back that she was thinking $750 but would take $550 for it. I just sent her the money to be done with it because I didn't want to tarnish the friendship, but I was pretty mad about the whole interaction.

MILA

on friends and money

CHAPTER 6

The Role of Friendships in Your Life

Each friend represents a world in us, a world possibly not born until they arrive, and it is only by this meeting that a new world is born.

ANAÏS NIN

The great thinker Andrew Sullivan recently wrote in *Love Undetectable: Notes on Friendship, Sex, and Survival* that the union of true friendship is far superior to romantic relationships. He says, "For me, friendship has always been the most accessible of relationships—certainly far more so than romantic love. Friendship, I learned, provided a buffer in the interplay of emotions, a distance that made the risk of intimacy bearable, a space that allowed the other person to remain safely another person."

His words got me thinking about our limited understanding of friendship in contrast with romantic and family relationships. This is curious, given that good friendships often last far longer than most romantic relationships, yet there are many more formal categories of thought surrounding romance. How quickly can you respond when your girlfriend asks for a status update on a new guy in your life? *He's the one. We're keeping it casual; it's just a hookup. He's a friend with benefits. I think he's just friend material.* Yet almost no thought goes into the levels of friendship in your life. Is your friend someone you see weekly? Is she someone you call every day? Is she someone you go on vacations with? Because friendships can take various forms, and those forms are our own creation, it's hard to know if we're doing it right. Lindzi Scharf, a journalist whom I greatly admire for many things, not the least of which is her ability to be intentional in friendship, shared with me: "I think I always thought of dating as being no different than friendship. To me, I have the same expectations going into both." This idea feels totally right to me. With people marrying later in life, if at all, the primary relationships in the character-building era of your twenties and early thirties are those with friends. Thus, it feels incumbent upon us to put these friendships front and center and really understand who means what to us and vice versa, not just so that we can take inventory but so that we can have clear expectations.

Facebook has so much to answer for, but perhaps its biggest crime is how "friending" has confused the very definition of what it is to be a friend. Seriously, how often do you see the majority of your social media "friends"? I see why the company chose that name, rather than "connection" or "network." It feels better, even if it's largely inaccurate.

This is not to say that every real friend should be a bosom buddy. We have the need—and the capacity—for all kinds of friendships. Aristotle wrote that there are three kinds of friendships: (1) friendships of utility, which exist between you and someone who has a use to you (and you to them); (2) friendships of pleasure, which exist between people who enjoy each other's company; and (3) friendships of the good, which are based on mutual admiration and respect.

Within those broad categories live a variety of other friendships. They all serve important functions in our lives. Each friendship you can enjoy, improve upon, or even just take note of adds to your well-being. Conversely, examining your friendships can shine a light on the relationships in your life that are just kind of there and not doing much for anyone concerned. Understanding what roles various people play in your universe is key to managing expectations. If I think we're best friends, and you think we're work pals, I'm probably going to get my feelings hurt. A key to this chapter is understanding that you can enjoy friendships at all different levels. They can all bring joy, fun, support, and well-being to your life, but they can also bring hurt and exhaustion your way if you haven't carefully assessed roles and expectations. All relationships are a kind of energy—and, as we know, they can contain positive and/or negative energy. And sometimes they contain both at the same time! But really getting your head around where and how you expend and receive energy is life changing.

You can think of the friends in your life as concentric circles, with acquaintances on the outer ring and your best friend as the bull's eye.

Acquaintances: The Outer Ring

These are people you're happy to see, but you don't book time with them. In theory, it's lovely to bump into them— at the grocery store, at an event—have a quick chat with them, and move on. These are also the people you interact with as you move through your day—the girl at your local coffee shop who knows how you like your flat white, the woman who runs the dry cleaning service you use, the owner of your dog's favorite playmate at the dog park. You might have friends in common. You like this person. But there's either not quite enough there to motivate you to take it further, or you haven't had the opportunity.

Social scientists refer to these kinds of connections as "weak ties." They might not be as strong as our more intimate connections, but they still affect our well-being in a major way. While the bulk of research has looked at close relationships, a study at the University of British Columbia in 2014 found that the more people interact with others they know but aren't close to, the more they report happiness, well-being, and a feeling of belonging.

I have to admit, I am pretty shitty in the acquaintance department. I'm the person standing in line to get my coffee and saying to myself under my breath, when the barista who regularly serves me makes eye contact with me, *Please don't talk to me, please don't talk to me!* Does this make me a jerk? On the surface, probably. After all, I was one of the few people who saw a silver lining in wearing masks during quarantine: the ability to go incognito! But after reading the study above, I realized something about myself. I am a far more guarded person than I need to be. I have to leave the house, right? I *want* to leave the house. So why not make the effort to connect each day rather than recoil? If I think about it, standing there desperately clinging to my precious time and energy, arms crossed, eyes bouncing all over the room to avoid making contact, I must seem full of self-importance and fragility. This doesn't mean that if you've lost your job this morning or been dumped, you have to be Miss Congeniality, but all things being equal on an average day, connect. *Choose connection.* As long as I (1) categorize these interactions as relationships, which they are, it gives them power and energy, and (2) make sure there are boundaries in place (i.e., I won't have a twenty-minute convo with a barista with each cappuccino I order), I have created intention and positivity in my world on a regular basis.

Acquaintanceships can't replace close friendships in our lives, but they do make our lives better. The social justice movement of recent years has introduced the word *micro-aggression* to the vernacular. It's used to describe the small, yet frequent, indignities and slights people of color experience. As that concept was disseminated, it began being used for these types of chronic injustices to many disenfranchised groups. People are willing to take part in nasty online trolling of those they don't even know. Videos go viral when a "Karen" throws a fit over a parking spot she's decided is hers. At the risk of oversimplifying these complex issues, lack of human connection is at their roots. Whether it's the product of systemic racism or the cyber veil we live behind, these are dehumanizing behaviors. Being willing to have small, but warm *human* interactions in your day-to-day life makes the world better, makes your life better, and makes *you* better. In a nutshell, even with weak ties, when you are intentional with these relationships, you reap and sow many rewards.

Middle Friends: The Middle Ring

Vivek Murthy, former surgeon general, wrote *Together: The Healing Power of Human Connection in a Sometimes Lonely World* after speaking to hundreds of Americans about how friendships, or lack thereof, were affecting their lives. In an article for Bluezones.com, Murthy explains the value of "middle-circle friends." He writes, "In this social region, we may not necessarily know one another's deepest secrets, but we enjoy having our lives intersect. Middle-circle friends provide a vital buffer against relational loneliness." As I discussed in chapter 1, loneliness and the absence of connection are not only sad but also have devastating effects on our health.

Although often dismissed as "less than," middle friends are kind of amazing. Because we make these friends mostly through work, hobbies, memberships of all kinds, and other such activities, they can be made fairly easily. And because they don't need to be profound, you can enjoy them without doing deep-dive emotional work. They come in a few different shapes and sizes.

HYPHEN FRIENDS (MOM-FRIENDS, SOCCER-FRIENDS, SCHOOL-FRIENDS)

You've probably had this experience in the past. You start at a new school or job, or maybe your kid joins a new activity—whatever the scenario, you're suddenly spending a big chunk of time with a new crowd. And you like them. They're pleasant and friendly. Maybe you even create a few in-jokes. You carpool each other's kids. Sometimes you even spend time together outside of work, class, or the sidelines of a soccer game. You're more than acquaintances, but it doesn't quite feel like a full-on friendship.

These situation-based relationships are friendships of utility, as Aristotle said, and are often described that way. According to Suzanne Degges-White, they act as a kind of social lubricant—they're enjoyable and practical, but they're not that deep. You don't sidle up to another soccer mom one Saturday afternoon and announce, "I think I'm in love with my husband's best friend!"

"Motherhood is a really profound stage for friendships," says Degges-White, and I can back her up on that. Particularly when you have your first child, you're so hungry for both information and support that it becomes practically essential to have mom-friends. It's someone to go on walks with when your baby will only sleep in the stroller. It's someone to text a photo of the rash you're worried about. It's someone to clue you in to the least embarrassing mommy-and-me activities in the neighborhood. And maybe you create a bond that continues long term, but there are so many reasons it likely won't. Your kids don't really like each other. One of you goes back to work, and the other doesn't. Your kid decides she'd rather play hockey than do ballet.

To dig into this phase a little deeper, I spoke to Michelle Kennedy. In 2017, she launched Peanut, an app that connects like-minded women at various stages in motherhood from trying to get pregnant through having school-aged kids. I asked her what makes mom-friends so particular.

> Something crystalizes in motherhood, where you
> need to have shared experiences. You need air time
> to talk about topics that you might ordinarily not
> talk about because they might be considered too
> taboo or too graphic or too boring. Outside of
> motherhood you'd have to get into a very close
> relationship to be able to have that conversation.
> It was your best friend who you were going to
> talk with about your sex life. And all of a sudden,
> you're a mother, you've got a two-week-old, and
> you're talking to a mom friend about the fact that
> you can't ever imagine having sex ever again.

Within the category of mothers, of course, there are many subcategories. Baby-led weaners, cosleepers, and go-with-the flow moms versus schedule advocates. And, maybe you've heard, people have *feelings*. Early motherhood years can be intense—your identity might be shifting, you're deciding what kind of mother you want to be—*as you're doing it!* And you are bombarded with opinions and judgment. *How dare you not breastfeed? You cosleep? You allow screen time? You have a nanny?* It goes on and on. And it's all so personal. "Peanut came about because I was meeting women, and they weren't my people, and there was something quite isolating about it." So, Kennedy created Peanut as a way to find *your* kind of mom in your area.

Elise Loehnen told me that for her, functional friendships really came into play as she evolved with age and life experience: "You create a whole new set of friends based around your needs, not necessarily your desires. One day, you wake up and you have these other, different types of functional friendships where the threshold is like, 'Who would I not mind spending a couple hours with on a Saturday at the park with the kids?'"

It's worth noting that it's likely that if your situation changes—you finish a course, your kid switches from karate to ballet—these friends might be downgraded to acquaintances.

WORK FRIENDS

We spend a lot of time at work—almost as much as we spend doing any other single thing—which means the people we work with are the ones we spend the most time with. And yet there remains a belief that relationships at work should be cordial but not close. In fact, many managers actively discourage friendships at work, assuming they will reduce productivity. In fact, research shows that happier, more connected people are markedly more productive. It makes sense: If work is a tense, emotionally cold place to be, how much will you want to be there? How creative and productive will you be? You certainly won't be volunteering for overtime. You likely won't feel compelled to help a colleague with a project.

Shasta Nelson starts her book *The Business of Friendship: Making the Most of Our Relationships Where We Spend Most of Our Time* with that ripped-from-reality-TV tagline, "I'm not here to make friends." Her book and a mountain of research make the case for exactly the opposite. People with friends at work are happier, healthier, and more productive.

Far from being a distraction, solid work friendships bolster performance. From a basic level, feeling happy and relaxed at work—as a result of liking your workmates—means you'll be able to be more creative. A lack of friendliness, in any setting, encourages people to keep to themselves. You're unlikely to offer an off-the-wall idea when you know you'll be met with disinterest or derision. But if you feel that your workmates genuinely like you, you're going to be more willing to offer your real opinions and thoughts.

Nelson reiterates the friendship triangle she established in her book *Frientimacy*. She posits that every relationship is built on a triangle made of positivity, consistency, and vulnerability. The more of each of these elements that exists in a relationship, the closer to the pinnacle of what she calls *frientimacy* it will be. That's the case whether you're looking at your ride-or-dies or the yoga teacher you see every Sunday morning. Some relationships will happily remain low on the triangle—you're happy to see your hairdresser and always have a nice chat during your cut and color, but you're never going to call her at 4 a.m. with a crisis of faith.

Work friends are likely to be somewhere between these two extremes. Because of the amount of time many of us spend at work, the consistency piece of friendship is baked in. If you enjoy people's company and like collaborating with them, the positivity requirement is also met. The vulnerability aspect of Nelson's triangle is likely the moderating influence. You might feel comfortable enough to give your work friend honest feedback about her presentation or know she'll have your back in meetings—but you might not get into deeply personal issues. And that is completely appropriate.

When you think about what's going on at work—literally a group of people taking on a common purpose—it makes sense that we become personally connected with our colleagues. My friend Sunny Hasselbring told me, "I find a lot of camaraderie through work that has fostered lifelong friendships. It's really important that I'm around people in a working environment that I like because it's a team activity."

So, there's no saying that a work friend can't come to have an important role in your life. I know many people who joke about their "work wife" or "work husband" because they've become so close to someone through work. My good friend Michal Steel counts a colleague as one of her closest friends. She met Audrey at a creative agency in Los Angeles. When Audrey made a change to a new industry, "She said, 'You need to come do recruiting with me!'" Ready for a change, Steel took her up on it, and they've worked together since 2015. "We have a great relationship. I wish for everyone to have a working relationship like the one I have with Audrey. We couldn't be more different. She's so type A, super buttoned up, and I think that's what makes her successful. But I am just not like that, and that's what makes me successful. There are different methods to the madness, but we have a deep respect for each other's process."

Friendships made at the beginning of a career can be particularly intense, as any relationship you make while you're changing can be. Loehnen remembers her time at *Lucky* magazine, and the friendships she made there, fondly:

> I made really enduring friendships, primarily at those early jobs. When you're in your early twenties and you're adulting and for the first time you're out on your own—you're no longer confined to college cliques. It seems like those have been some of my richest friendships, friends that I made at *Lucky*, when we were trying on our adult personalities for the first time. We were getting our hearts broken and figuring out how to go out for dinner when we were all living paycheck to paycheck. I don't know, there's something about that that was so fun and bonding.

Men have always cultivated warm relationships at work—and have reaped the benefits of them in the form of the old boy network. Does the notion of "using" friends to get ahead make you feel uncomfortable? Is it hard to believe you can have genuine affection for someone and accept or offer professional help? A criticism of many powerful female boomers is that they had to work so hard to accrue power and then didn't pass it along.

Being a good work friend means being willing to spend some of your personal capital on others rather than hoarding it. This can take the form of throwing shine on a colleague's ideas in meetings, offering to connect two work friends who might be useful to each other, or suggesting someone for a job. Remember, happy work wife, happy work life!

Having said all this, one of the things I noticed throughout my career is how easy it is to become friends with someone at work by commiserating over negative aspects of the job. It's amazing how quickly you can bond with someone over what a jerk your boss is or how disorganized the whole company is. And it feels so good to let it all out and to hear that you are not alone in your suffering. There are big problems with this, though, if you don't pay attention. Entire relationships can be based on negativity, and this negativity inevitably seeps into your subconscious. Secondly, these conversations can become self-fulfilling prophecies, in that you can become actively toxic without even realizing it. In other words, *you* are contributing to the negativity of the place now instead of being a force for good or simply focusing on getting where you need to go, career-wise. I will admit, there is something about these friendships that feels so good in the moment—the venting, the jokes, the gossip, the release—but if that's all they are, you have to see these relationships as limited and limiting.

I'll never forget when I first started my career in the startup world, at pretty much the bottom rung of the ladder. I didn't know anyone at the company when I started. But after being there for about three months, I began taking an occasional lunch with a coworker who seemed cool. We had certain things in common, and we liked talking about fashion and comedy, but we hadn't really *gelled*. One day, after a particularly brutal meeting, we headed out of the office to eat our Subway subs (all we could afford!) in the sun. A couple of bites in, I blurted out, "Is it just me, or is our boss an absolute ass?" Well, from that second on, the floodgates were open—I mean *geyserville*. She immediately chimed in with six examples of his assy-ness, including a specific description of his socks that day, which were also offensive, and we just never looked back. From then on, we always ate lunch together, G chatted throughout the day, and sometimes even texted funny memes or random workplace thoughts on the weekend. At one point I counted more than twenty texts that ended with the hashtag #SundayScaries, coming off of a fun weekend and into another week. I thoroughly enjoyed these interactions. They were entertaining, and they reduced the stress of a new job in a new industry. The problem was that the complaints seemed to take on a life of their own. The truth was that I was actually doing pretty well at the job. Certainly, our boss was still annoying, but honestly, whose isn't at times? Then the day came that should have been a big celebration. I was called into my boss's office. I was nervous at first—could he have seen my G chats? But quickly it became apparent it was good news: I was being promoted, in a big way. Now I was going to be running the small department I had just been working for. I was excited and proud, until I had to share the news with my friend. Then I became almost embarrassed. That day at lunch I told her the news, and she said . . . nothing. Crickets. I was now going to be the manager of the very organization we had been demeaning for almost a year. The whole exchange was awkward. And practically just like it had started—in a frenzy—it shuttered. I was surprised and hurt. The loss left a real hole in my work life for a while. We tried a couple of times to grab a bite together, but it was never the same. We had let the negativity be the base of the relationship, and without it now, we had nothing. It certainly didn't have to go that way—we had a lot in common on many other fronts, but we leaned in to what felt good and kind of scandalous, and as a result, we lost the friendship. It is so tempting to take refuge in the gossipy, low-hanging fruit of a work friendship, but when that's its primary foundation, it is doomed from the start.

Power imbalances can play a role in which work friendships are going to be successful. Obviously, fewer politics are involved between friends at the same station in a company. But there's no reason employees and bosses can't be friendly. Nelson points out that people will leave jobs because of their supervisor, because of terrible office politics, because of feeling undervalued and disrespected. Being friendly with your bosses allows them to know more about your goals and your potential. If you're the boss, building a friendly atmosphere of trust means that employees will come to you with challenges early rather than hide them until they blow up. But notice I'm specifying *friendly*. There must be boundaries between management and employees.

Kennedy recalls a work friendship that ended badly. "I had a very, very close friendship in my former life, where probably I felt quite maternal to her. When it didn't work out for a variety of reasons, it hurt so badly. And that is just a place that I never want to get to again. It has to be more of a surface friendship, not like living each other's lives, families entwined. It doesn't work."

COUPLE FRIENDS

It's a rare couple friendship that doesn't start between two people and then their partners get woven into the mix. If you and a close friend both get into more serious romantic relationships, it's natural to at least see if you can double date. And don't worry about everyone being equally close—it's almost never the case. It's okay if your girlfriend and your bestie's husband enjoy the time you all spend together, but don't ever make plans for just the two of them.

One of the key benefits to having couple friends is that they reinforce the very notion of being in a committed couple. It's also an opportunity to be up close to another romantic relationship, allowing you to consider what you would like to or not like to emulate about the way that other relationship functions. You might appreciate the way a friend's husband makes a big deal out of her accomplishments and remind yourself to do more of that in your own relationship. But you might also notice the way a friend rolls her eyes at her partner behind his back and make a mental note to resist that urge yourself.

SITUATIONAL (TIME AND PLACE) FRIENDS

These are friends you see regularly but infrequently: at summer camps, family reunions, annual vacations, or work retreats. These relationships, while not part of your everyday existence and not part of your tried-and-true support system, can provide great value to your life. They allow you to explore different sides of yourself that you might not put on full display or even have access to in the rough-and-tumble of daily life. While these relationships mostly happen in childhood, they are certainly possible at any stage of life. The fact that these relationships exist outside of your norm often allows for more freedom and, if you're paying attention, can offer the opportunity for self-exploration.

Each summer, I used to go to the lake for a couple of months ("Oh, Canada!") and had a small group of really close friends there. Each year, it was as if no time had passed, and I dove right back into my friendships. With those friends,

I had created small businesses (selling slushies to passing boaters), held talent competitions (one of my life highlights was lip-synching George Michael's "I Want Your Sex" to the horror of our onlooking parents), experienced my first foray into alcohol (stealing alcohol to create "shit mixes" consisting of gin, rye, vodka, etc., all in one mason jar), and skinny dipped. I still look back at those experiences as not only some of my happiest but also my most foundational. And yet, we didn't make a single phone call to each other from September to the end of May. It was only when one year my mom suggested we invite my "lake friends" to my birthday party that I froze—a weird sensation coming over me. I was fraught with anxiety and tried to suggest that my party was better as it was every year, with my *school friends only*. My mom insisted, and so it went, a mixed affair. And as predicted, it was a bizarre experience. None of the magic was there from the lake, and I found myself almost hiding out, at times, to avoid mixing my friends. Needless to say, I had a terrible birthday, and for a moment it made me question my lake friends, until the following summer, when we fell right back in again, hot sweaty bodies launching off the dock into the cool, clear water, screaming and laughing. It was only years later, as I reflected upon that fifteenth birthday party, that I realized why it had been so awkward. Through my different groups of friends, I had honed different parts of myself. Through school it was all about academics and popularity, and through my lake friends, it was, actually, a much more vulnerable side of myself: the risk taker, the fearless explorer. When these two groups met, it created a level of self-exposure I simply wasn't prepared to navigate. In fact, my reaction at the party to my lake friends' presence hadn't been rejection but protection. I was protecting them, along with that vulnerable part of myself.

These time-and-place friendships can be an exciting way to develop something new in yourself. You're away from your day-to-day life, but you also usually have more time with these friends when you are together. I spent nearly every minute of those summers with my friends. When you vacation with a group of women, you have days to get into things, to try something new.

Friends as Family

Living with roommates is usually considered a life stage to put behind you as quickly as possible. During college and for a few years afterward, living with friends is fun and economical. You learn valuable life skills from each other, have someone to laugh with after a bad date, and have a pal to watch reality TV with on nights in. As soon as we're able, via an increased income or a romantic relationship that gets serious, we leave our roommates behind.

For a host of reasons, some women are taking another look at sharing a home with friends. Not everyone wants to get married or find a partner; or they did get married, and it ended in divorce. Women tend to live longer than men, and if you're healthy enough, why wouldn't you choose to live in a home with friends rather than a senior living community? Cohousing is an alternative to intergenerational living—which for myriad reasons doesn't suit everyone—that many women are considering for many of the same reasons they did in their youth. It's cheaper, and it's more fun. There are many ways this can work. In 2019, Ikea presented the Urban Village Project with the aim of providing a better quality of life through modular construction with different configurations for families, singles, or friends. In 1998, six women launched Older Women's Co-Housing (OWCH), and now twenty-six women between fifty and seventy are living together. Many organizations around the world pair older empty nesters with students as a way to address housing shortages. And my favorite example was reported on the Cut. Seven young women in China made a joke pact that when they turned sixty, they would move in together to enjoy retired life. That was 2008. Just ten years later they decided to go ahead and make it happen much sooner. They designed and built a stunning home that offers the right balance of private and shared space, including a pool and a tea pavilion.

Best Friends: The Inner Ring

These are your people. You've put in the time, you've allowed yourself to be seen, you've made mistakes and fixed those mistakes. Lots of friendships are great but never reach the center. But the prize for the ones that do is enormous.

Essential to this level of friendship is the exchange of seeing and being seen. There is simply no intimacy without it. A former employee of mine for whom I have great fondness, Branche Foston, talks about it in terms of safety. She worked with me at LEAF, and we've stayed in touch since; she's gone on to become an entrepreneur herself. She launched the Honey Block, a wellness startup for millennial creatives and entrepreneurs of color. She says,

> I think for me what defines friendship is for sure safety—both people feeling safe with each other. I feel, truly, in my close friendships, the people that I'm friends with know that they are safe to show up as themselves. They are safe to be honest with me about things. They are safe to check in with me about my behaviors and report what they aren't feeling comfortable with. I think, I mean as cheesy as it is, it's just that genuine support. I think it's shown now more than ever with the uprisings and the pandemic that you have to have people who are in your corner. It doesn't necessarily have to be in a public way. But who is checking in on you? Who is safe and can really see you?

It doesn't have to be serious, either. Your closest friends can show how well they know you in all sorts of ways. Sasha Tong describes the teasing humor that binds her six-pack of friends.

> We all rail on each other, in the most loving way, but it's fucking hilarious to us too. I don't think everyone is cut out for that. Like, I'm a very time-oriented freak of nature. I need everyone to be on time, and I want everything to happen early. Duana is always late. Always. Always putting on another outfit as she's walking out the door. Lainey is heartless. We know who we are, and we make each other well aware. But in a funny way.

In talking to women while researching this book, I found several people whose best friend lives in another city. They all made time for calls, FaceTimes, and/or Zooms and made sure to prioritize trips to spend time together. Maria Menounos told me about a time her husband prescribed a visit with her best friend, Alyssa.

> In my pre-brain-tumor time, when I was working like a crazy person, I would get really, really sad, and I didn't know what was wrong with me, and my husband would say, "You haven't seen your friends. You haven't seen people to re-charge you. Go see Alyssa or have Alyssa come in." And it would make me feel better instantly. Because you forget in your hamster wheel and you just start going, going, going and you don't realize how massively important connection is, not just work. I started to realize those cycles, and then I started setting alarms for myself to remind me, don't forget, this is important too!

HOMEWORK

No matter where the people in your life fall in the concentric circles of friendship, they should all have merit and meaning. Being thoughtful about who's who in your world can help you better adjust expectations and energy output to give the best your most and the rest enough.

- Make a list of your friends by category. For example, list your work friends, couple friends, best friends, and so on.

- Do your expectations of time and closeness for each friend match with her category?

- Is there anyone you'd want to move to a different category?

- Are there any big holes?

I had the same issue with two friends. And it was very crazy.

I moved to Los Angeles from France for work. I hadn't made a lot of friends for various reasons. But Jen was in Los Angeles, I met her, and she was my closest friend when I arrived in the country. She was working in my agency. She is French as well. I had another very good friend, Julie, who lived in New York. They met each other through me.

Both had been trying for a long time to have a baby. Julie had been trying a really long time, and nothing had been working. Finally, Jen ended up moving to New York, and they ended up becoming very good friends and bonding because of their struggle.

Around that time, I had started to have the conversation with my partner about maybe trying to get pregnant as well. I had some health issues, and my doctor said that I had to have surgery. After the surgery, the doctor told us it was going to be difficult to get pregnant or take a long time, so I didn't even tell my friends that we had technically started trying. And then all of a sudden, like immediately after starting to try, I was like, "OMG, we're pregnant!" I was really shocked.

I didn't know how to tell my two friends. I knew it was a real struggle for them, a real source of pain. So, I just called and told one of them straight out, and she immediately called and told the other one, and after talking, they both said that it broke their hearts that I didn't share that I was even trying to get pregnant. And both kind of agreed they couldn't talk to me anymore. It was so hard. Literally, one of them called me and said, 'I'm sorry, I can't talk to you.'

And honestly, I felt so bad, and I understood how hard it was for them and how it must have felt unfair that for me it wasn't hard. But in the meantime, I felt very alone, very hormonal and emotional, and it was very hard for me. It felt very lonely to have lost these two people.

About two years later, Julie came to L.A., and she still wasn't pregnant, but she called me. We met up, and I was with my nine-month-old daughter. It was as if no time had passed. She said to me, 'I'm so sorry. I want to be friends with you again; I miss you.' So, we tried to work on things. It was then we started having a really honest conversation.

We talked about the five years that she had been trying to get pregnant and what she had been going through. She was living in New York; we were seeing each other often; I was going to New York often for work or she was coming here. She was trying that whole time, and I guess I just couldn't understand what that meant. I was single, I didn't know anything about how it must feel. But I think, at this moment, she was trying to find people like her who were trying and struggling because there is something—it's like a different language being spoken in this situation. I think that's why she gravitated toward Jen. But anyway, I just always felt like I didn't know what type of questions to ask, and I felt it was such a sensitive topic.

When we started to be friends again and talking through everything, she said to me, 'You didn't ask me any questions . . . you were my closest friend, you didn't ask me any questions about how I felt.' And I was really surprised. I felt I had honestly been there for her, but maybe not in the way she needed? I told her, 'Honestly, I didn't know what to say. I thought I was trying.'

We continued to talk through this crazy, sad event, this moment in our lives. It was really hurtful. I was so sad—it turned out in some way that on this one, I was part of the breakup. It was not just 'Oh, you have a baby, I hate you.' It was more like: it's been a long time, I'm waiting for you to be more invested in my issues right now, and you don't ask me, and so you have a baby now. Okay. I'm done with you.'

It hurt, but we talked everything out and now we are closer because of it. And both moms. It was a really hard thing to go through.

I have never heard from or spoken to Jen again."

EMILIE MEDOFF
on friends and fertility

CHAPTER 7

Friendship Diagnosis

No person is your friend who demands your
silence or denies your right to grow.

ALICE WALKER

What came to mind for you when you saw the title of this chapter? Does it sound like I'm asking you to judge the worthiness of your friends? Make a list of who goes and who stays? Or does it make you think of how you might see shortcomings in your relationships in a way that gives you the chance to improve them? Does the whole idea seem kind of cold?

We know friendships are extremely important to our well-being, in almost every way. Or, at least, they can be if we nurture them. In order to reap those benefits for ourselves *and* provide those benefits for others, we need to bring attention and awareness to our friendships. We need to know ourselves and our needs, be responsible for meeting those needs ourselves first, and then see how those needs are being met in our relationships.

How Do You Feel?

The first part of the assessment I'm asking you to do is about time and energy. Who are you spending time with? For the next four weeks, keep track of all the people you spend time with. Include coworkers, family, friends, your Pilates instructor, your babysitter, other carpool parents. You get the idea. Get into the habit of noticing how you feel when you interact with each of these people. Are you at ease? Anxious? Guilty? Inspired? Uplifted? Do you feel like yourself? As we discussed in chapter 4, not every moment spent with people has to be rainbows and sunshine to have value. But if there's someone who has recently left you feeling bad about yourself or just deflated, look back further. Is that bad feeling a one-off, or is it a pattern when you are with that person?

Don't worry, you're just collecting data at this point.

How Do You Behave?

The second thing I want you to take note of is your own behavior in relation to all the people listed above. How do *you* act? What's your reaction to seeing her number flash on your phone? Do you have to cancel three times for every time you actually get together with her? Do you drop everything when you get a call from her? Do you suggest grabbing a quick coffee, or do you insist on dinner so you have more time together? Do you have lots to say when you're together? Are there subjects you avoid with a certain friend? Is there a friend with whom you're prone to overindulge? Do you find yourself trying to impress some friends? Do you like how you behave with them?

Again, no judgment; just pay attention.

What Role Does Everyone Play?

The third part of diagnosing your friendships is looking at the role each friend plays in your life (and the role you play in theirs). We've already looked at the different kinds of friends we can have—friends at work, friends in activities, friends in conversation, and so forth—but it's also essential to consider *the way* each friend affects you.

Tom Rath, director of Gallup, conducted a large-scale study of friendships and their importance. In *Vital Friends: The People You Can't Afford to Live Without*, Rath encourages a friendship audit to evaluate what relationships are providing you and find ways to improve those relationships based on their strengths.

One of the most compelling concepts in Rath's book is the notion of "rounding error" to describe our tendency to expect the people in our life to be perfectly well rounded. In reality, it's just about the best way to ruin any relationship. Just as in romantic partnerships, if you expect your best friends to be well rounded enough that they meet all of your friendship needs, you're likely to be disappointed. Expecting friends to contain every quality we need leads to focusing on what they *don't* bring to our relationship. If you believe your friend should be hilarious, wise, supportive, connected, and insightful, but in reality she's only three of those things, you're likely to focus on what's missing. Rath's research found that people who focus on what's missing in friendships eventually start to have negative feelings about them.

Analyzing both what you need in friendships and what various friends provide you actually allows you to give up unreasonable expectations and enjoy your friends for who they really are. If you're aware that it's your friend's intellect you most value, you're able to lean in to that aspect of your relationship. You can imagine your friendships like a Venn diagram; each circle can't contain everything you need, but in the overlap of those friendships you can get it all. It's important to note that you and a friend will likely have a reciprocal but not equal relationship—meaning that perhaps you turn to her for her rock-solid work advice, and she comes to you when she needs to blow off steam with a night out.

If you Google kinds of friends you need, you'll see that most lifestyle websites and magazines have a spin on this. According to Rath's research, there are eight vital roles friends can play in our lives. I've seen motivational speaker Stacey Flowers give a TED Talk about the five types you need in your life. The point is, we are multifaceted beings, and it takes a friend village to meet our needs.

Considering what I need in a friend group, I thought about how I want to feel as well as what I need (whether I always want it or not). My own Avengers include the following superheroes.

THE NOSTALGIC FRIEND

This is someone with whom I have history and memories. We shared a cabin at summer camp. We sat beside each other on the first day of college. We were interns together at our first jobs. This is the person who knew us back in the day, well before we were fully formed adults. She knows about the stupid things you've done for love and the ways you were in her corner when it counted. These kinds of friendships don't always require a ton of upkeep, unless you want them to be a big part of your current life. When you see these friends, it's like no time has passed. And for me, the biggest value they provide is grounding you in who you really are, in the purest sense.

Remember my lake friends? Well, one of those friends is named Marnie. We spent every summer together from birth until around twenty years old. We have seen some shit together. We grew up together in those summers (including, among other things, drinking, smoking, and playing spin the bottle, away from the watchful eyes of our parents). I have probably seen Marnie only a handful of times over the past twenty years. But each time, I'm left feeling like magic. I just don't laugh with other friends the way I laugh with Marnie. I am tickled to the core reminiscing about the pickles we used to get ourselves into, or some of the weird crushes we used to have. I am instantly elated when I remember moonlit trips out into the bay to stare at the stars and sip hot chocolate, shushing each other as our giggles echoed across the water. When I am with her, I feel innocent again, just for a moment. And man, does that have power. These encounters also help me remember my Canadian-ness (and could I use some of that now, mid-COVID, mid-Trump, mid–life crises!). Also, there's just no way I could bullshit her.

THE NURTURING FRIEND

This is the friend who knows what you need. You can walk into a room, and she knows there's something bothering you. She texts some encouragement when she knows you're about to go into a tough meeting. You can be real with her about your challenges, but she's not only in it for the drama—she cheers your successes too. This friend makes you feel safe to be vulnerable with her. True nurturers are there for all of your feelings, but it can be easy to turn to them only when things suck. Be sure to balance your relationship with fun as well as venting.

It can also be easy to forget that nurturers have needs too. Sasha Tong is a producer on *etalk*, an entertainment TV show, and cohost of the advice podcast *What's Your Drama*. In her friend group, she's known as the fixer. If friends are struggling, they know Tong will listen and then lean in with advice for how to make things better. But when she faced a serious health crisis a couple of years back, she got a rude awakening. She saw specialist after specialist to figure out why she had constant pain in her eyes. Unable to diagnose her, they told her she'd likely have to live with it for the rest of her life. On finding a natural solution, she laughs, "Of course I went the wiggy route, and I was able to turn it around, but those were dark-ass times." The real shock, though, was how few friends reached out to support her. "If I'm being perfectly honest, I would say about 90 percent of my friends let me down." She realizes now that the experience led her to depression. And her disappointment in her friends turned to anger, which she had to let simmer down before communicating her feelings to them. "I've learned that I do need to speak up more when I do need something. To say, 'I need you in times like this; I can't do it alone.' So, I think it made my friendships better."

She's also come to realize that being her gang's go-to for advice means she has to pay attention to her own well-being. "I do have people who trust me and trust me with very precious things about their lives. And sometimes that can be very heavy. So, I do have to make sure that my mental health is okay."

THE CREATIVE FRIEND

Just spending time with this friend fills your head with a million ideas. She's smart, but her real gift is making you feel *your* smartest or most inspired. Your conversation crackles, time moves quickly, and you leave your time together feeling uplifted and energized. This friend is a doer. TV host Tracy Moore says one of her friendship strengths is the encouragement she offers. "Even though I'm a major realist, I like to help people dream a little bit. Like, 'Let's see how this might unwind. Let's actually plan this.' I'm a planner, and I will help you plan!" This kind of friend is a powerful ally at any stage of a project—in the beginning when you need validation for your ideas, when you're midstream and need bucking up, and at the end when you need to have your accomplishments cheered. Their problem-solving abilities also make them great collaborators.

THE MENTOR FRIEND

This person might be your senior, but not necessarily. Whether she's older or younger than you, girlfriend has *lived*. You need her take on the important decisions in your life. You'd never take a job or start a major project without going over it with her first. She's got your best interest at heart, and you never feel like she might be competing with you. Be sure not to take this friend for granted. It's easy to fall into the habit of calling on this friend only when you're in need, but that would be a mistake. It's not that she doesn't like helping—she does—but she has needs too. Let her know when you've taken her stellar advice and how it worked out. Mentors take pride and pleasure from knowing they've been helpful. Be diligent in asking about how her life/work/romance is going so you don't create a lopsided friendship.

THE FRIEND LIKE YOU

We like to be with people similar to us. Sociologists call this *homophily*, or "love of same." Researchers in many arenas have looked at why this is, and the answers are complex. A study from the University of Royal Holloway–London showed that participants felt that people they thought looked like them were trustworthy. The *Journal of Social and Personal Relationships* released a study that showed we're drawn to those with whom we have a lot in common because (1) they confirm our opinions, (2) we're confident in being liked in return, (3) we like the same things, so we have fun together, (4) after we have positive feelings about some characteristics, we begin to fill in the blanks and assume more positive attributes, and (5) we see an opportunity for growth (even though someone unlike you is probably a better candidate for helping you grow).

This can be a simple and straightforward proposition. You meet someone, and you both love French cinema, running marathons, and talking politics—amazing! Then you learn you both grew up in strict Catholic homes in the Northeast. Oh, my god, you have so many shared experiences! If you're temperamentally aligned, it's hard to imagine not becoming fast friends with this person.

This category really hits home for me. Two of my best friends in the world, Kayleen and Larissa, are Canadian like me. We all moved down to Los Angeles (separately) more than a decade ago and are totally connected through the shared experience of struggling to make it in the United States while being super homesick for our native land. Beyond just this, even though English is spoken in both countries, it's almost like we have our own secret language when we're all hanging out together. A deep-rooted Canadian-ness. We see the world the same way, and it seems much different from those around us. Our sense of humor is from the same place. Our values. Frankly, without these two women in my life, I don't know how long I would have lasted here. Anytime I feel lost, a call or a drink with either or both helps get me back on track. Especially going through this unbelievable political cycle, I can't tell you how many times we've checked in with each other: "This is crazy, right? I mean, is what's going on crazy, or am I crazy?" "No, this is legit crazy. It's not you!"

Thinking about how mobile our society is now, things can start to get tricky. Rarely do people grow up in a town or city and never leave. We're not surrounded with people who are just like us for all of our lives. Now add systemic and under-examined racism to the mix, and it becomes complex. As diverse as North America is becoming, it's still easy for white people to live and work in mostly white spaces and therefore let that feel like the norm. Many people of color have, by necessity, learned to navigate in primarily white spaces. And if I didn't know it before, the last year of social justice protests has made me think a lot about the importance of space for friendships within marginalized communities.

Remember my young friend Branche Foston? She told me about how she appreciates having different friend groups. "I realize how privileged I am because my cup overflows in abundance of love from the friendships in my life. And how lucky I am with having these different friend circles. There are times when I don't want to be around a cisgender, heterosexual male, so let me go be around all my queer friends and flourish, or there are times where I need to only be around a Black person for the next forty days. I feel that's the beauty of having these pockets."

Although Moore has many white friends and colleagues, she definitely values time spent with Black friends:

> There is an easiness that comes from being able to say, "Oh my gosh, I'm just having problems at work because my supervisor keeps talking about my hair," or you know, a couple of my close friends are teachers, and they can talk about some of the students and how they're being treated because of their race. I mean, these are things that literally come up in every conversation we have, and it's not because we're race obsessed, it's because race is a major issue in everyone's lives. So, it comes up all the time, and there's an easiness. There's something to be said for not having to explain everything. No one is saying, "Are you sure it's about race?" Everyone is saying, "Okay, how do we deal with this?"

There is much value in the comfort and understanding that comes with friends who are like you or come from the same place you do, but you also want to watch that you are not creating an echo chamber. Anita shares,

> I think sharing values is important in a friendship, especially when they are healthy values such as honesty, concern for others, humor, determination, and

respect. But sharing values is different from surrounding yourself in a bubble where everybody just agrees with you because everyone is the same and afraid to not be like the other members in the group. You like the same music, wear the same clothes, grew up in the same neighborhood, have similar education or jobs. In that situation there is not much learning going on; instead, you are making yourself feel powerful based on numbers, not necessarily based on anything of real value. Feeling vulnerable or like an imposter is not uncommon for women, and having a friend or belonging to a group of friends can be an easy answer to developing real self-confidence from achievement and growth. There are some women who attain a high level of confidence using power. A very good friend makes me laugh out loud when anyone asks her if she was ever a cheerleader; she always replies: "I don't cheer for other people; they cheer for me." But many women don't have that kind of confidence. My friend is one of the kindest people, but that kindness comes from a feeling of inner strength and hard-earned confidence. The reality is that many people who have put in the work to earn their own self-confidence also have the capacity to be generous to people who are different than they are. But when we use our friends to pump up our self-esteem, we have to cling to our female circle much more tightly and tend to exclude others because when our friends aren't there, we don't feel good about ourselves. Friends can help us feel powerful, and that can be important, but when people are mostly using friendships to cope with feelings of inadequacy rather than trying to overcome those feelings, they lose out on some of the real advantages of having good friends that challenge us to grow and learn.

THE FRIEND NOT LIKE YOU

For all the reasons stated above, it can feel really good to have a friend or friends like you. But for all those same reasons, it's not a good situation if *everyone* you know is like you. In contrast with an echo chamber or a bubble, simply put, diversity in your friendships reduces the opportunity for prejudice. It's much harder to make negative or inaccurate assumptions about someone you're spending time with and become fond of. Becoming close with someone from a different culture, a different life experience, a different socioeconomic class—all of these friendships also give you a chance to question your beliefs and assumptions. For people outside of the dominant culture, this is probably already happening. Black women are used to navigating white spaces. Queer women are used to navigating straight spaces. People in the dominant culture need to stretch themselves to adapt to new situations rather than expecting others to bend. As big of an opportunity as diversity in friendships represents, you never want to make someone feel like a token or a step on your path toward wokeness. And be prepared to make mistakes. There's so much fear around being cancelled these days that people can withdraw from trying. It's okay to make mistakes as long as you're willing to own them and keep evolving. Again, my young friend Branche, with all of her wisdom, says,

> If you are a white person and your life is homogenous,
> bless yourself by making your life as open and colorful
> and fluid as possible. Of course, in a respectful way. I
> see some of my friends I grew up with, and still every-
> one looks like them. I'm still their only Black friend.
> I'm like, yikes. I really hope you can get more fun and
> happiness and joy and beauty in your life because there
> is so much to learn from all these other people and
> experiences. Not like it's people of color's job to teach

you. Do it in the most authentic, loving way possible. The more that you expand your life, the more that you really will become the person that you want to be and are meant to be. You'll love to deplatform and decenter yourself. You'll be happy to do those things. I joke with my friends, 'If I'm the most fluid, radical Black person you know, then yikes, yikes, yikes!' I was like, I can give you a list of like fifty people who are way more progressive, cooler, creative, Blacker, whatever you need. I can be the little gateway drug, but there are far more people you need to be having in your circle. I'm like your Diet Coke. Don't let me be the one Black person you have. I'm proud of myself, I love myself, and there's so much more that you could be calling in.

THE VITAL FRIEND

You might also know her as your best friend, your homie for life, or your ride-or-die. If you're lucky, you might have a couple of these friends. If you call at 3 a.m., she's picking up. Dead body in your living room? She's helping drag it out. You're making an epic mistake? She's risking your anger to give it to you straight. This kind of friendship requires attention. You can't expect to receive the gold standard of friendship if you don't invest time and energy.

Important disclaimer: Your list might look different than mine. But it's worth your time and thought to know what yours is. Ask yourself: What do I really *need* from the people in my life? Many friends will have more than one role in your world. A best friend might be creative, nurturing, and vital. A friend at work might only be creative. An older sister might be a nurturing mentor. And you might be entirely different things to each of these friends. Getting to know how friends fall into these categories means you can lean in to the strengths of those relationships, you can manage your expectations, and you can really grow your appreciation for them. Gratitude between people strengthens their bond. Let your friends know explicitly what it is you value in them. It doesn't have to be a Hallmark moment, if that's not your style. But people like to know that they're doing things well. So, let your nurturing friend know, "Thanks for listening to my freak-out last night—it really helped me get it out." Or text a mentor friend: "You were totally right—my boss wasn't hinting I shouldn't apply for that job. In fact, she wants me to!"

Think about your friends. What roles do they play in your life? Ask your friends what role you play in theirs. Are there missing pieces? Can you evolve a friendship so it speaks to more than one or two of your needs? Approaching all of these questions with curiosity rather than judgment is important and will make you feel less gross and more empowered about it.

Toxic Friends

It's important to recognize these kinds of relationships for one reason and one reason only: so you can end them. Toxic friendships can often be old ones. If you met these people as an adult, you'd likely not form a close bond with them. At least, I hope you wouldn't. But maybe this friend who seemed like a lot of fun at school has developed some very nasty habits over time. Or maybe you just weren't paying enough attention to realize she's really not a friend at all.

Signs you're in a toxic friendship:

- They only call when they need or want something
- The conversation is never equal
- They put you down or make fun of you in front of other people
- You feel bad about yourself after you've spent time with them
- They are aggressively competitive

- They aren't happy for you when good
  things happen to you, and you hesitate
  to share good news with them
- They bring drama to your life
- They bitch about you behind your back
- Your relationship is built on conditionality
- They bail on you
- They use your secrets against you and share them
- They are a bad influence and encourage
  you to do things that get you in trouble
- They talk about other people behind their backs
- They exclude you from things with mutual friends

And here's the rub: A person behaving in these ways is surely creating the toxic relationship, but make no mistake, if you are tolerating these behaviors for any length of time, you are the cocreator of the problem. You are complicit. They are the parasite, but a parasite can't survive without a host.

There's a catch: Toxic people are often super, super fun. And charming. And hilarious. There's something about their unreliability that makes them feel special when they do show up. Or do something selfless. Or compliment you. But it's a trap, I'm afraid. You can give a confrontation a whirl, and you can absolutely try to establish some boundaries to maintain your emotional safety with this person. But it's unlikely you'll be able to—safely!—be close to this person. If you're a nurturer by nature, you might feel pulled to fix this person, but if she's not coming to you asking for help, it's unlikely to work.

I remember, quite vividly, one of my more toxic relationships. It was slightly different than a classic toxic relationship in that she never made me feel weak or bad about myself. In fact, she was effusive in her praise of me: *"I don't know what I'd do without you!"* She was a talented, super fun hairstylist with her own shop who, for one reason or another, *could not* get it together. At least once a month, there would be a huge drama in which she'd call me crying and need my help. You name it, landlord kicking her out for some wacky reason, physical altercation with an ex-boyfriend outside of a bar, her cat needed a rare surgery for $3,000 *or she'll die*. Everything felt like life or death, and she needed my life-line. With each instance, I'd jump into full savior mode and problem-solve until either she calmed down or the problem went away, and I'd be deemed the hero once again. And then just like that, she'd text me the next day like nothing had happened. Totally normal, like, "Hey, did you watch *Housewives* tonight? SO good." It was nuts. I'd be emotionally exhausted from the night before, and yet she was good to go. Not surprisingly, this started to take a toll on me, and I tried to become a little more distant, but when a person who is crisis-prone feels you pull away, what happens? Moth-to-a-flame kind of shit. She felt inescapable, and I really felt like if I abandoned her something bad would happen to her. Finally, there was the last straw. She had been in some major drama with a boyfriend, and she left the house and needed a place to stay. I had a tiny back house that was empty at the time, so I suggested, with great hesitation, that she could stay there for a couple of days. Two weeks later, I needed to get something for work out of the house and texted her that I needed to come in. She didn't respond, and finally the next day, needing to get the stuff, I quietly went back there. I knocked; she wasn't there. I entered. The house was a full disaster. Two weeks' worth of dish-es were piled up in the sink, rotting spilled milk was left on the counter, dog hair was *everywhere*. I could not believe my eyes. I was furious. As I stood in the filth, I just remember thinking, *This girl will never get her shit together*. It was over. I sent her a text saying I had family coming to stay in three days, and she needed to find another place. She didn't respond until three days later, when she simply texted: "I'm out." I went to the back house, assuming she had at least tidied up a bit. Nope. All I got for a thanks was that sink full of dishes and decaying food. We never spoke again. At the time it was easy to dismiss this as good riddance to a crazy person. Certainly, I learned one of my great life lessons out of the experience: If there is an unbalanced person and a sane person, the sane person always thinks she can help the unbalanced person find a little more balance. What happens—every time—however, is the unbalanced person succeeds in making the sane person a little (a lot) less balanced. Looking back on this story, however, there was so much more there. This relationship was feeding my ego, my need to be important to someone, perhaps my need to feel a little more sane in my own shoes, and by comparison, I did. I was totally complicit. How much better would it have been for me to directly address my own needs or vulnerabilities than work them out through someone who was clearly unbalanced? Is that harsh? Maybe. But these types of situations with people are often teachable moments. We need to fight the inclination to keep patting ourselves on the back for all we are giving and take a closer look at what we're taking. What void are these situations filling in your life?

What's Your Style?

The final step in the diagnosis is to understand your friendship style. Are you a one-on-one friend? Or do you prefer groups? Do you like to be active in some way when you spend time with friends, or do you prefer sitting across a table with a glass of red wine and lots of conversation? Think about *how* you like to be with friends. What are the times that you've felt the most supported, connected, and lit up with friends? That will lead you to understanding your friendship style.

Journalist Lindzi Scharf prefers her friend time to be one-on-one. "At my baby shower, I had so many girlfriends in the room together, and none of them knew each other." A self-proclaimed empath, Scharf says, "I think people have always energized me or drained me. Because of that I never spend time with someone I don't really want to see. I don't like small talk. I want to be able to have real conversations."

My friend Michal Steel is the opposite. First of all, she has a lot of friends. Like, the most friends of any of my friends. And she makes an effort to maintain all of them. I was surprised by her reaction to me describing her that way. "What? I don't have that many friends. Well, I guess I have groups of friends." She then went on to describe her work friends, her client friends, her couple friends, and her core close friends. You see what I mean.

Tong also rolls in a group. Her friend group is made up of six women she stays tight with via ongoing text threads and regular dinners. Busy schedules mean that sometimes only three of them can get together. "It always works, but the best time is when we're all together. I find when all of our personalities come together, that's when the magic happens. It's not to say that if it's not all of us that it's not fun. It's just not the same, and we've always tried to create that group setting so that no one is left out. If you don't, you feel like you're walking with a limp if you don't have the other person."

Knowing your friendship style will help you avoid feeling out of sync with friends. If you have a friend who is always trying to keep you out late going to one more crowded, noisy bar, and your style is more morning walks, you're going to have some low-level tension.

She might feel like you're bailing early because you're not having fun with her. You could feel like she doesn't really want to talk to you when you can barely hear her over the music, unless you communicate, of course. You could tell her, "I love hanging out, but I'm just not my best after 10 p.m. I know you love going out, so let's find a compromise that works for both of us. How about brunch this Sunday?"

HOMEWORK

I hope you are starting to see that so much of friendship really is about you: who you are, what you need, and what you can give. It's about doing the upfront work of understanding the intricacies of what makes you *you* so that you can bring the fullest human being possible into relationships. This might feel self-centered. How can the starting point of relationships be about me? The point is that as you work to become evolved and in step with yourself, you will start to demand the same in your friendships. You will actively seek out others who have done the exact same type of work on themselves (or at least have the desire to start), bringing the fullest version of themselves into relationship with you. This is where connection really has a chance to light a spark that keeps both of you warm for as long as you both are game.

- Make a list of your close friends.

- Beside each name, note the qualities you enjoy in that friendship. For instance, are they nurturing, creative, vital friends? Or are they nostalgic friends who are like you?

- Again, are there holes in your list? Perhaps you're missing a friend who isn't like you? Maybe you could use a mentor friend? Think about where you might find that kind of friend. (Book club? Running club? Joining a team?) Be intentional in seeking out who and what you need!

"I've known Fay for as long as I can remember. She's the daughter of my mother's good friend. She is the same age as my older sister, so she was friends with my sister before she was my friend. But Fay is a sweetheart. She didn't talk down to me, and I felt like she was my friend too.

In the tenth grade, I attended an all-girls Jewish day school in Brooklyn, New York. Away from home and boarding in another family's home, and I wasn't happy, so I started acting out.

I did not do well in a number of classes. Two months into the school year, I was expelled. Private schools do not accept new students mid-semester. And I was not a great student at the time. Who would want me? I felt sad, humiliated, and angry.

At that time, Fay had become the director of a small private K–8 day school in Palo Alto, California. Mom called Fay and told her what happened. Without skipping a beat, Fay said, 'I could use an assistant in our preschool. Adele can come here!' I don't know if she actually did or whether she was wanting to help. It didn't matter.

In the blink of an eye, I went from Brooklyn to sunny California!

The job as a preschool assistant was a dream job for a young high schooler like me. The kids I taught adored me. The parents and community accepted me lovingly. I went from feeling like an outcast to feeling valued and appreciated because of Fay. She kept an eye on me and, of course, we became close. I truly believe Fay rescued me from a very different destiny. She was a good friend to my mom, my older sister, and especially to me.

ADELE BEINY

on how friendship can change your life

"I have a very good friend—we used to do everything together. Traveling, late-night texting, date recapping. We were really two peas in a pod, but also, we have a friendship within a tight group. But me and her were the last two single ladies standing, so there was a kind of different language spoken. And then, after years and years of searching, my guy (now my husband) landed right in my lap when I was least expecting it. We met and never looked back. But the hardest part now is the group dynamic. Like we're on all these group texts, and everybody is talking about double dates, dinners with husbands, etc., and she always chimes in, 'So is anyone going to invite me because I'm not married?' And it's really hard.

She's in a really bitter state right now. I was just watching an episode of *Sex and the City*, and it's really describing her. But she's just in an angry phase. At first, I was really defensive with her, but I totally get it. I was the "Last of the Mohicans" with my friend, and now it feels like I'm gone too.

We went all over the world together. We really had the best time together. We'd have happy hours, go out. She was the last person we had over here for dinner before the lockdown. It makes me sad because I think she's awesome. She's not resentful toward me, but I think, as a whole, our group chat is all married girls. I feel bad, but what do I do, just cut her out of the group text? Start another group? That feels like I'm validating that she just doesn't fit in.

It's tough to see because, you know, you love someone so much, and you want them to succeed in that department.

I don't lie, and I don't personally feel like I'm on egg shells around her, but I think, as a collective group there's a sense that now things are a little awkward."

SHIRA
on transitional life phases within friendship

CHAPTER 8

How to Become a Better Friend

Wishing to be friends is quick work, but friendship is a slow ripening fruit.

ARISTOTLE

How are you *doing* friendship? So many of us expect friendships to just exist happily. The truth is that many of us simply take our friendships for granted. Either we've shared some deep experiences over time or have known each other forever and haven't taken the time to do more. We're content to accept the status quo because we're mostly unaware that we could do better or be better. If we have the urge to do more, we often rationalize that our lives are too busy to invest more effort or attention. Just because there might not be anything *wrong* with these friendships, we consider them *good enough*. Or we feel ho-hum about a friendship, and we decide, *Well, that person isn't a close friend.*

To my mind, this is a missed opportunity. A wealth of experience, meaning, and depth lies right at our fingertips—something we need now more than ever as the digital abyss disconnects us further—and yet we skate right over it. The truth is, like anything worth having, real friendships take work—but results far outweigh the investment. What keeps people from real change is not just effort but fear. To forge real connections, to have the kind of intimacy with another that inspires growth, change, and joy, you have to be vulnerable. Really vulnerable. And this doesn't sound all that appealing to many of us.

Another problem is our understanding of what friendships should be. We think they should be all fun, all closeness, all support. As a result, at any sign of a problem, the conclusion we might incorrectly jump to is that the friendship is no good. Because we're told that friendships should just *be*, we don't think of them in the way we think of family or romantic relationships. Most of us know that we have to invest in our family and our romantic partner for those relationships to thrive. But there's no equivalency with friendships. If they require work, we consider them defective. As a result, we luck into great friendships, accept good enough friendships, or ditch imperfect but perhaps salvageable friendships.

And so, there's a world of friendship opportunity being missed. If we value our friendships and honor all of the ways they improve our lives, we should be willing to invest in them—not just because they're broken but because they can always be deepened and expanded. We can become better friends and have better friendships.

In chapter 4, we looked at the anatomy of a strong friendship—the pillars of what must go into great relationships, or they simply won't work. In this chapter, we're looking at how they operate or, rather, how *you* operate within a friendship. What are the healthy friendship habits you need to practice to give and get the most out of friendships? What are the friendship moves you need to master to grow your friendship superpowers?

The first part of being a better friend is an inside job. There's a theory in child development called *attachment theory*, a term coined by John Bowlby in 1958. Until then, scientists had underestimated the bond between parent and child. The theory goes that a close, loving, and safe bond between parent and child creates a secure attachment style. If a child is ignored or emotionally abandoned, an avoidant attachment style might emerge. An ambivalent attachment style can be created by a highly inconsistent emotional relationship between a caregiver and a child. And most dysfunctional is a disorganized attachment style, in which children are raised in chaos and trauma.

Okay, why am I talking about attachment theory of early childhood in a book for grown-ass women? It all goes back to knowing yourself and your needs. Your attachment style certainly still affects you. The emotional atmosphere in which you were raised has neurological, and therefore emotional, consequences that will be part of all of your relationships. Of course, this is not to say that you can't learn and grow—you most certainly can. But it's valuable to know your starting point.

As always, I encourage you to think about this with a sense of curiosity rather than judgment. Discovering that you have an avoidant attachment style doesn't mean you're destined to be the needy half in any friendship. But if you know you require a lot of emotional reassurance, you might as well put it out there to the people with whom you hope to be closest. If a friendship is made up of one person with an avoidant attachment style and one person with a secure attachment style, it would be helpful to have an explicit conversation about it. Now, before you barf on this book, hear me out.

My parents are amazing. I'm lucky to have grown up in a household that was loving, supportive, and structured. As a result, I recognize that I have a secure attachment style and—outside of extreme situations—I rarely feel jealous. If I have a friend who had a bumpier start, who developed an ambivalent attachment style, and who gets upset if I'm even a minute late for our coffee date, I could easily feel weighed down. I might feel unfairly judged. But if this friend had the self-knowledge to say, "I know it seems like I'm obsessed with promptness, but it's just an old trigger," I'd feel such empathy for her that I'd either never be late again or be sure to text her if I'm running late.

After you're aware of your attachment style and how it affects relationships, you can start acquiring the habits that will improve your friendship powers. When I interviewed my great friend and psychology colleague Jette Miller for this book, she brought something to my attention. She is always putting together fabulous little get-togethers or small adventures, and I am one of the lucky ones who's always on her invite list. The problem is, with a two-year-old, a looming book deadline, and my thesis on the horizon, I have RSVP'd "no" probably 85 percent of the time. During our interview, she reminded me of the time she asked me about it. "Do you remember when I asked you if I should stop inviting you to all of the events?" I replied, "Yes, vaguely." "I think I followed up with saying something like, 'I don't want to put unnecessary pressure on you.' But that really wasn't the problem. I think my feelings were starting to get hurt." Now she had my attention. I remembered replying, at the time, something like, "Not at all! As long as you don't mind me saying no, then invite away!" and then hearing nothing more. "When I reflected back on it," Jette said, "I know that I have a kind of abandonment anxiety, or a fear of rejection. As you know, both my father and sister died suddenly, within a very short time of one another, and it instilled a fear in me that anyone I cared about could leave me at any time. I think I sent out all of these invites looking for a confirmation that you wouldn't leave, but I wasn't getting the response I needed to hear." I was truly stunned. I felt like a total jerk. Of course, I couldn't have really seen the direct connection without the conversation, but certainly she had sent a signal that in retrospect warranted further inquiry. What's more however, this new exchange between Jette and me did more to further our relationship than any other incident within our friendship. We had the beginning of deep understanding of how the other needed to function and could work on being aware and fully honest.

Healthy Friendship Habits

LISTEN ACTIVELY

You'll sometimes hear someone described as being a "good listener." What does it mean, and why do we even need to point out that someone is a "good listener"? Well, because so many people suck at it. At best, we're thinking about what we're going to say next rather than listening to what's being said. At worst, we're scrolling on our phones while people talk to us. In both cases, we're not hearing what's being said, and we certainly aren't understanding what is truly being communicated. Remember, truly listening to somebody isn't just about hearing words and being able to recite them back verbatim. There are so many other nonverbal cues that help inform us about what is really being said. These are easy to miss if we're not totally present in the moment with the other person.

There are obvious ways of becoming a better listener, such as making eye contact and not interrupting. Subtler practices are nodding and giving small encouragements in the form of "Umm-hmm," "Okay," or "Right." Paraphrasing back what you've been told allows your friend to correct you if you've gotten it wrong and shows that you're paying attention. You can use phrases such as, "What I'm hearing is . . ." and "Sounds like you're saying . . ."

Clarify when you're confused with phrases such as, "I want to be sure I understand you . . ." Or "Do you mean . . . ?" Resist the temptation to tell the story your friend's story makes you think of and steer the conversation over to you.

But the most important aspect to active listening is the most counterintuitive. In describing listening, Doug Noll, author of *De-Escalate: How to Calm an Angry Person in 90 Seconds or Less* and founder of Prison of Peace, says, "Don't listen to what is being said." That's right: Don't listen to the words. Rather, pay attention to the emotional information being communicated. Is your friend tense? Fearful? Sad? Then reflect back what you've taken in.

Practicing active listening builds trust in friendships and makes it more likely that your friends will come back to you when they need to talk next time. You're not just taking in information; you're letting your friend know that she's worth listening to and knowing. Feeling seen for who you are is an essential component of friendship. It's not surprising, then, that multiple studies show that people who practice active listening are considered more socially attractive than those who don't.

Finally, active listening is not only important as a skill but also important to demand from your friends. The listening must go both ways. If it doesn't, there's a lot of room to grow here. Set yourself up for success. If you've got something heavy or sad you want to share with your friend, don't just spring it on her. You could text before you call: *Do you have fifteen minutes today? I really need to talk about something.* Now your friend can find a window in her schedule when she won't be distracted. And you've let her know you're not just calling for a quick check-in; you need her to be ready to listen.

COMMUNICATE

The flip side of active listening is communication. To become closer to someone, you have to share yourself. You can't truly be seen if you don't communicate who you are. It doesn't have to be your deepest, darkest secrets, but it does have to be the things you care about. Tell your friend about a book you fell in love with, what you think about current politics, how you feel about an upcoming trip to visit your in-laws. And if it is heavy, don't hold that back either. Journalist Lindzi Scharf told me about a time a friend shared a difficult experience only after it had passed. "I asked my friend why she hadn't shared it earlier, and she replied, 'Oh, I didn't want to burden you.' I was really taken aback. It's not a burden for a close friend to share something she's going through. It's almost like I'm insulted if you don't want to share it, if you don't want to burden me with what's going on in your life. That's what friendship is all about."

BE DISCREET

This should go without saying, but don't assume you know if a friend's story is for public consumption. No one is going to make themselves vulnerable with you if she knows you dine out on her stories. It's also not for you to steal her thunder by telling friends her big news. My friend Anne told me about a time when a friend she'd cowritten a book with told Anne's recent ex-boyfriend about their book deal. "I couldn't believe it. It wasn't like I wasn't speaking to him. Of course, I had wanted to be the one to share that news. I know she was as excited as I was about it, but I felt kind of ripped off by it."

PRIORITIZE FRIENDSHIPS

It's just so easy to send a text and cancel. I used to be the queen of this. How many times have I jumped for joy when I get an email from a friend saying, "So sorry but I've got to reschedule!"? YIPPEEEEE. But you have to put in the time and effort. Sometimes that reaction of relief is a sign you need to reevaluate the friendship, but sometimes it's a sign you've dropped the ball. We always hear that marriage takes work or that kids take work, but for some reason friendship is just supposed to be easy. We can look to friendships as a break from the heaviness of other relationships or responsibilities, but friendships are like anything else in life; you need to invest in them if there's going to be any payoff. When I talked to Shasta Nelson about this, she used a metaphor that made me laugh. "If you only go to the gym once a month, you're not going to see results. It would be a mistake to say, 'See, it doesn't work!' You have to increase consistency to see results." After a long work week, it can feel like just one more obligation to meet a friend for brunch—but you are almost always glad after you're there laughing over coffee and eggs.

CREATE RITUALS

Set up consistent activities that are "your thing" with a friend. Establishing and maintaining rituals helps fortify a relationship and makes it feel special. There's security in knowing you can look forward to something with a particular friend. Lainey Lui and her best friend, Fiona, live in different cities. One of the ways they stay connected is taking trips together. "With Fiona and I, walking is our thing. We went to Nashville a couple of years ago, and we'd walk twenty kilometers one day, thirty the next day. And when you walk with someone, you can't put on your headphones—it's so rude! We plan walks, and we talk the whole time."

Besides just being really nice to share with someone, rituals can have a restorative element. In talking with my friend Jette, she described their importance:

Rituals around relationships are often shared among friends without great awareness. When life is balanced and uninterrupted by reshaping events, these rituals come easily to us—yoga classes, mani-pedis, hiking, movie nights. Rituals around friendships often help us cultivate healthy behavior and support us in our personal growth. Friends inspire new explorations and widening of the experience horizon. But when there is an interruption in the flow of a friendship—one of the friends is undergoing grief, divorce, childbirth, taking care of an elder—it can get out of rhythm. Bringing awareness to your rituals with another can help fortify them and you when life gets in the way. Rituals can keep us connected and grounded when life unroots us.

The most bonding of all activities is singing. Robin Dunbar says that any form of exercise done with a friend will give you a boost of endorphins. Synchronized activity increases the benefits we feel. And singing or dancing together, which requires cooperation and close attention, is significantly more satisfying to us than mellower hobbies such as crafts. This might explain the enormous popularity of Toronto's Choir! Choir! Choir!, a drop-in choir that meets weekly to sing mostly pop songs. They've been singing since 2011, and the videos they post on YouTube almost always go viral. You don't need to join a choir if that doesn't feel right, but think about the elation you feel belting out songs while driving with a good friend.

ALLOW FOR MESS

We have this unfortunate belief that friendships should just be perfect. And if they're not, the other person must be a bad friend. Or we're the bad friend.

In romantic relationships, we communicate hurt or disappointment. It's not easy, but there's something of a road map for it. You let your significant other know that when she leaves her dirty laundry on the floor, you feel like the maid. You tell your boyfriend how it makes you nuts when he takes a phone call during dinner. "I always say that we feel closer after we've gone through those conversations," says Nelson. "Because now we feel like we can trust them, and we've been through something together. And yet we never give our friends the same gift."

Lui agrees. "As much as female friendships have been celebrated, and that's definitely a good thing, we have done friendship a disservice by making it seem like it's this organic magic that doesn't require practice."

My friend Jette adds, "I think the problem is that there's no culture around conflict. It's just been parked in the romantic relationship department. There's no language between friends, and there's no fast resolution. So, when something comes up, it has such a weight. It gets misinterpreted as a really, really big deal because it so often doesn't happen."

"I've cancelled friends for too-small things before," says Chriselle Lim, the influencer you met in chapter 3. "Now that I look back on it, I probably shouldn't have cancelled people that quickly. It should have been about being accountable and learning from your mistakes and having that conversation and getting better. It should be accountability culture, not cancel culture."

We undervalue our friendships by insisting they only be about good times. Giving a friend a chance to do better by you, or giving yourself permission to do better by your friends, allows for growth and complexity. It can be scary to admit that someone has hurt your feelings, but it gets easier when you follow Brené Brown's rule of assuming that people are doing their best. And rupture and repair—as we've discussed earlier in the book—is essential to building strong, complex friendships.

BUT NOT TOO MUCH

I'm not telling you that you and your friends can't have a bitch session, but I am telling you to pay attention to how those sessions leave you feeling. If you are constantly in a negative gossip loop or a drama cyclone with a friend, it is time to evaluate how this relationship is leaving you feeling. Whenever Nelson speaks to large groups, she asks the audience to self-evaluate which plane of her friendship triangle—positivity, consistency, or vulnerability—represents the biggest challenge in their friendships. She finds that people always state that consistency is their number one challenge, which makes sense—we're all busy, and finding time for friends is tough. However, she follows up with a more thorough intimacy quiz, and the result is entirely different. Positivity is consistently the lowest score.

Her theory is that while we're acutely aware of the calendar and how long it's been since we've seen a person, we're less focused on how we left them emotionally. Do your friends leave your get-togethers feeling a buzz of that friendship high so many people report? Magic. Wildness. Different women have described it in different ways—but it all comes down to that great feeling we can get and always crave when it comes to friendship. Or do you leave them depleted?

This is likely why people suspect consistency is a bigger issue in their friendships than positivity. Nelson says, "If I go to a happy hour with someone I see every few months and I come home like, yeah, that was okay, and my brain isn't saying that was amazing, I can't wait to see them again, then I'm not going to be consistent because it didn't give me anything meaningful."

It's normal and important to allow for friends' moods. If your friend is getting divorced, you're not going to hold it against her if she's not making you laugh. But if there are no underlying reasons for a friend's bad attitude, and you don't feel like you can address it, you've got a problem.

BE CAREFUL IN TRIANGLES

Friendships within groups are common. And so are the complications they seem to breed. It's all too easy to call one friend to vent about the other rather than get real with the friend with whom we're upset. You might get an immediate sense of relief from your bitch session but (1) the problem is not solved, (2) now you've involved someone else in the problem, and (3) it's just a shitty thing to do. It's harder but more valuable to be direct. Remember my friend Sunny Hasselbring, who learned from her childhood experience to talk to others rather than the person at issue directly? "I learned to have a conversation with somebody else about the person—and not the person I should be talking to. I had a friendship breakup that occurred as a result of this exact behavior. It doesn't mean that I was in a healthy relationship and wish it had continued. But it actually ended because I talked to somebody else about the person, and she found out."

BE AWARE OF DIFFERENCES

It's human nature to believe that our experience is a typical one. Several studies have looked at various aspects of this phenomenon, and it is known as the *false consensus effect*. Basically, it goes like this: If I'm willing to cheat on an exam, then I'm likely to think that cheating is normal or at least common. If I have knowledge on a subject, I believe that this knowledge is commonly held. This is a particularly powerful drive if you live in a community of people mostly like you because you might have little experience with people unlike you. When confronted with evidence that consensus does not exist, we often assume that those who do not agree with us are defective in some way. Looking at you, Facebook. It doesn't help that the notion of "alternative facts" has been disseminated throughout our culture. This is just one of the ways living in a sameness silo can be damaging to our friendships.

When I asked Lui for the most common friendship dilemma, she and *What's Your Drama* cohost Sasha Tong receive, her answer really surprised me: "We get a lot of questions about friendships between people who belong to a different class. Like, 'My friend wants to go on this holiday, and I can't afford it.'"

It reminded me of a story my friend Leslie had shared with me. In her early twenties, she was living with another mutual friend, Rachel. They were both just starting out in their careers, hustling, and having a great time. There was a third friend in the group, Sara, who came from wealth. "The three of us would make plans to go out, and Sara always wanted to go to these expensive Hollywood restaurants, and we were like, 'We can't go there! Our parents aren't paying our bills.' And she'd be like, 'Oh, I'll pay for it, then.' She just didn't get it. The money thing became really awkward. I mean, how many times do I have to tell someone I'm broke? It became a real problem."

Beyond finances, there is a whole world of differences to pay attention to. Who needs reminding of the triggering effect of different political views right now? Different upbringings can create a whole different set of perspectives that factor into a relationship, specifically around conflict or celebration. Really understanding the entirety of the other person can help make so much room for deepening the relationship or help resolve issues. Not paying attention to these differences can have the opposite effect. You might easily dismiss this: "Oh, I know so-and-so was born here and grew up there . . . " but do you know how those experiences *resonated* with her, shaped her, and show up in your relationship? Have you communicated your own experiences in a nuanced way that furthers understanding and empathy?

BE THERE UNTIL YOU CAN'T

We've all watched in horror as a friend has made a choice that we know will end in disaster. And maybe not for the first time. It's painful! When you care about friends, it might be easier for you to see the pothole they're about to drive into, and, of course, you want to warn them. But this is probably one of the trickiest zones of friendship. How to know when your friend needs an intervention, a piece of gentle advice, or for you to shut the hell up?

First you have to consider the stakes. Is she buying a sweater in a color she loves but that, in your opinion, fits terribly? Unless she insists on knowing your thoughts, shut the hell up. If you suspect her boyfriend is abusive and she's in danger? You absolutely run a loving intervention. But of course, most situations exist between these two extremes.

Next, find out if your friend wants input. We all know that sometimes the most satisfying thing in the world is to bitch about a situation. Complaining can feel *so* good! Ask—explicitly—what your friend is after. Does she want your advice, or does she just want you to listen sympathetically? If you barge in without checking, you could advise yourself right out of a friendship. I know someone who had a come-to-Jesus moment with a best friend about her fiancé. She thought this guy was all wrong for her friend. She thought her friend could do better. Ten years later the couple is still married, and the friendship is done.

My friend Sunny told me she's learned how to walk the line.

> I think it's deeply important not to be judgmental of your friends. We might be able to say, "Ooh, that's a bad idea." But there's a caring and loving way to support your friends, even when you don't agree with their choices. And then if you were right about their decisions, you don't say, "I told you so!" You hope

that you will be wrong about your predictions. I've had to learn this lesson the hard way as I have been judgy.

When a friend was going through fertility challenges, Sunny tried her best to be supportive. It's not that Sunny thought this friend was making a mistake, but she didn't get what the big deal was:

> In my head, I was like "Oh, God . . ." I didn't
> understand what was hard about it. And then to
> have that experience myself later and have her
> be so incredibly supportive of me, it made me
> realize that life is long. And just because I don't
> understand something in the moment doesn't mean
> I'll be spared later. It's kind of like the golden
> rule: treat people how you want to be treated.

This isn't to say that you have to keep your mouth shut if you see a friend making a mistake. Sunny continued,

> You don't have to put blinders on in your friendships
> and not tell the truth. If you love somebody and
> you care for their well-being and you want to stay
> in their life, you have to learn how to have the hard
> conversations, lovingly. And I think once you've said
> your piece, that's it. You've done it. You can't make
> people feel attacked or backed into a corner. If you
> can't get over what someone is doing in their life,
> that's not the person's problem, it's your problem.

Tong has been on both sides of this dilemma.

> In my twenties, I had a really shit relationship. He
> cheated on me. It was really bad. He was a functioning
> alcoholic. And I had a friend who supported me in every

decision. If I wanted to work on it one day, she'd say, "Okay, let's do that. Let's try that. Let me give you some advice on how to do that." And the next day I'd say, "I want to leave." And she'd say, "Okay, let me support you in that. And we'll navigate that." And she almost subtly strategized, like through osmosis. She was guiding me, even though I thought it was my decision. She supported me in a time when I didn't have the answers. The door was open, and there was no judgment, at least to my face! It was important that she left it open because she knew it wasn't going to be cut and dry. Those situations rarely are.

And although Tong is known in her group as a fixer, she knows that she has limits.

If you're going to come to me with a problem, and you continue to come, time and time again, like year after year—at some point I do have a breaking point. I get bored of that. Because my advice will not really change. So, after a while, if they're just not taking the advice, I get irritated, and I think that's a bad friendship quality of mine. I don't think that's a good thing to do, but I will, at a certain point, say, "No, thank you. You can't bring me this problem anymore."

I think that's really fair. There's a loving way to let someone know that it's just too hard to talk about a situation over and over again and not see your friend try to make a change. It doesn't mean you won't be open to the discussion should things shift. And it's a gentle nudge that might actually help your friend make a move.

EXPRESS GRATITUDE
This might be the most important way to improve your friendships: express your gratitude for them. Many studies

have looked at the psychological and sociological bonds created through the expression of gratitude. When you acknowledge the kind deeds of a friend, you're letting them know you value them. In turn, when a friend notices your own kind behavior, you feel appreciated and recognized as a good person. It feels good to receive high marks for your humor, your good nature, your way with a martini shaker, your knowledge of 1990s pop songs, or what have you. And we want more of that good feeling. We like to be good at things. It's actually true that in expressing gratitude to a friend, you can improve your relationship *and* the odds that they will be even kinder to you! And while it's great to know that your friends are wonderful, this is a case where you really have to say it.

Testing, Testing

I sat down with my best friend, Sophie, to do the friend questionnaire below. Without question, she falls in the ride-or-die category in my life. Or put another way, during quarantine she was definitely in my bubble. We have had a long, winding relationship that started when I hired her right after she graduated college and had just moved back to Los Angeles from New York. Despite our ten-year age difference and the formality with which we began, we have become closer and closer over time. There was just an instant spark that we've kept on nurturing. Not having my own parents or brother in Los Angeles, she and her family have become my surrogate family, stateside. Being a successful jewelry designer, she also helps stoke my creative side, which I absolutely adore. On the one hand, this feels like a kind of magical relationship just meant to be. But the peril of that is we don't really feel the need to check in with one another about the relationship, and now that feels like a mistake or perhaps a missed opportunity. Certainly, we have had our small arguments, and we have our differences.

For example, she shares every emotion she's ever feeling, to a fault, and I am stoic to a fault, but we have gotten past our little challenges and moved forward. Ironically, Sophie was the last person I interviewed for this book, and when I realized that, it struck me. She should have been the *first* person I asked about friendship! So how did that happen? Was I taking this relationship and its magic for granted? Or did I simply know she would appear at any time to help me out, as the best of friends do, so I didn't need to prioritize her? So, when the idea of the friend questionnaire came to my mind for this chapter, I knew I wanted to do it with Sophie, not because we were in a rough patch but as a real check-in on the state of our relationship, together, after all of these years.

Sophie gladly accepted the challenge and late one morning breezed into my office, seven months pregnant and glowing. "So, are you going to hand me my ass, or what?" she laughed as she plopped down on the couch in front of me. Leading up to her arrival, I definitely had some apprehension. Would this be awkward? What would it reveal? But the moment she sat in front of me, I felt perfectly at ease. I think this moment might have been the most telling of the whole experience. Sitting in her presence, I knew that whatever might come up, we would be all right. This feeling should be a goal to set for every one of my close relationships.

I won't share the details of our session—that is personal—but I will say this: No matter how good or how bad the state of your relationship is, making the time to sit down and really do a deep dive with someone you're really close to, to pay that relationship its due, can only lead to something better. If only to provide clarity. If the relationship can't handle this type of honesty, is there really a relationship at all, or have you just been in a series of rudderless interactions with this other person? You can truly know only by asking the questions and being receptive to hearing the answers.

HOMEWORK

Though it goes without saying that trust and loyalty are fundamental to being a good friend, our behaviors most often can be improved. For example, you can be the most loyal friend in the world, but if you scroll your way through most of your get-togethers with a friend, you've got work to do. Like so much of what's been discussed, the awareness piece here is huge. Start by just witnessing how you interact with the people right in front of you, and this will probably be enough motivation to get you practicing the art of friendship.

Plan to sit down with your most important friends and discuss this questionnaire together. My advice is to do this and *then* go out for a drink, not the other way around!

- Name a couple of things you love about me.

- How would you define our friendship?

- Is there a specific moment you knew we would be friends?

- What is one of your best memories of our friendship?

- What are some of the things we have in common?

- What do you think are some of our biggest differences?

- When was the last time I irritated you, and you didn't say anything?

- Why didn't you say anything?

- When is the last time (if ever) you feel like I let you down or disappointed you?

- When was the last time I told you I loved you?

- Are there subjects you feel like you just can't discuss with me?

- Is there anything about you that I don't know that you want me to know?

- Is there anything you need or want from me that you're not getting?

- What's your friendship superpower?

I met my friend Yolande through her roommate Troy at a party in their apartment in Montreal when we were both really young. I think I might have been twenty or something, and she was nineteen. I had graduated and was already working in the fashion world, and she was still in school, just about to graduate. Anyway, we met, and we just had this big, wonderful energy between us. Like kindred spirits. Together with Troy we were the best of friends. When Yolande graduated, she moved to Paris for a year, and I missed her so much. And so we decided to start writing each other letters. It was the most amazing thing. She moved back after a year, but then it was my turn to leave. I ended up moving all over the world, first for my career and then with my husband for his work. But no matter where I went or where she was, we had a constant string of communication through these letters. They made me so happy. It was just the best feeling—this was long before texting and cell phones—to go to the mailbox and voilà, finding here this beautiful, perfect new letter from my friend. There was such intimacy in the letters. Like our own private world. And each time, until I found the letter in my box, I didn't realize how much anticipation I had built up. Just to see her handwriting on the page, her choice of words, it was like we were sitting together in a little bubble. And writing back to her felt just as nice, like journaling, but I really felt like I was being heard, not just talking to myself. It made me realize what was really important because these are the things I would want to share. That made me take stock of my life with each letter. We have written letters to each other for over twenty-five years. It truly is amazing. Now with texting and cell phones we chat much more this way, and the letters are fewer, but when we get together—I'll fly to see her in Montreal, she'll visit me in L.A.—we'll often reminisce about our exchanges. Last year we met in New York for a girls weekend, and she surprised me by bringing a couple dozen letters. We read them all aloud. Oh, my god! The stories we used to share; how different our lives were. Unbelievable, the memories we shared apart as young women, but now we're reliving them together as we read through the letters after a couple of glasses of wine. There is so much love in each and every one of them."

HELENE CORNEAU-COHEN
on rituals in friendship

CHAPTER 9

How to Break Up
with a Friend

About a year ago, I was having lunch with Laura, a new friend I had met at my son's school. She was originally from Belgium and fairly new to Los Angeles. She was also a writer and struck me as being really cool. As I sat chatting with her over coffee at Zinqué café, we began to discuss what projects we were working on. I started telling her about this book (still very much in its infancy), when Laura exuberantly jumped in, "Oh, my god! I love this. I just had a breakup with one of my friends last year!" I paused, then said, "What do you mean? Like, an actual breakup?" She looked confused: "Well, yes, isn't that what you're talking about?"

Now, up to that point, I had considered a friendship breakup in a more metaphorical sense. I hadn't conceptualized an *actual* breakup. My jaw dropped: "Tell me everything!" Laura went on to detail how over the course of a year, she and her friend Jessika had grown further and further apart in their interests. Yet, Jessika remained insistent on making plans. The more Jessika wanted to get together, the more resistant Laura felt. When the two did get together, there was little to discuss. Laura left every meeting feeling guilty that she hadn't tried harder to connect. Finally, frustrated by always feeling guilty, she decided to talk to a third friend about the situation. When she did, she learned that the same friend had also been a confidante to Jessika. Apparently, Jessika had been really bothered by her unrequited interest in the friendship with Laura. It was then that Laura decided she needed to end the friendship.

"How did you do it?" I asked, squirming in my seat.

"Just like I would with a boyfriend: I called her up, asked her to meet, and said we needed to talk."

"And?" I asked, on the edge of my seat.

"When she got there, I just explained how I was feeling and told her I thought the relationship had run its course. I told her I didn't want to hurt her feelings, and I know I had been by not being upfront."

In the end, they parted ways, Jessika feeling sad and maybe a little confused. But Laura felt a sense of relief and confidence that she'd made the right decision for both of them. What impressed me the most was not only Laura's self-respect but the profound respect she had for Jessika and friendships generally. She wanted the relationships in her life to be the best for all parties involved. And to Laura, that meant sometimes having to end an old friendship. She felt strongly that this benefited all of her other friendships—she had more time for what was really working, and she was willing to protect what being a great friend meant.

As I sat with this story, I reflected on the idea that all things must end—even life itself. And in light of this, doesn't it make more sense to have some control over the ending of a friendship and pay the experience a little respect? Why not move on, as opposed to leaning in to laziness, fear, or not-so-blissful ignorance of a friendship that isn't working? Like anything with meaning in your life, such as breaking up with a lover or quitting a job, endings are often hard and uncomfortable, but these simply aren't good enough reasons to avoid them. Swimming in mediocrity steals your power and your creativity.

So, why is it so taboo to break up with a friend? So much so that we frequently ghost people we want to be done with rather than face the discomfort of ending things explicitly. The big question I often get is not about *if* someone should end a friendship but *how*. The truth is that there isn't *one* way to end a friendship. Every relationship—including its end—is unique.

However, there are some consistent factors to consider as you face a potential breakup. It's not a straight path from friends to not friends, but I've created something of a map.

The first thing is to be sure that this is what you want and isn't some knee-jerk reaction to having hurt feelings or built-up frustration. As noted in earlier chapters, there is much to be done here before taking that final step. Perhaps your friendship needs an adjustment rather than an ending. Ask yourself if you could improve the friendship with any of the healthy friendship habits outlined in chapter 8.

Likewise, if you feel a friend pulling away, you can't always assume it's because you're being ditched. While researching her book *Toxic Friendships: Knowing the Rules and Dealing with the Friends Who Break Them*, Suzanne Degges-White talked to many women about their experiences. She met a woman who felt a friend slipping away. The woman's calls weren't being returned, so she decided to confront her friend about it. Degges-White recalls what the woman told her about the conversation: "She said, 'I feel like you're not there for me the way you used to be. And I'm really worried. What is going on?' And the other woman said, 'My husband was diagnosed with cancer a month ago. I didn't want to share it with anyone. I didn't want to bring everyone down. I've been wrestling with it.' And this woman realized that inadvertently her friend was driving away the support that she needed more than ever." Both women were hugely relieved to have the truth out in the open.

Another consideration is how a troubled friendship falls within your network. Is this friend part of a friend group? What will happen to your Pilates-then-brunch-self-care-Sunday club if you decide you're done with one of the four members? Will your wife be devastated if you can't have dinner parties with a certain couple because you no longer want to be close with one of them? Being part of a group might work to soften the edges of conflicts. If you're part of a five-woman friend group, you can lean in to conversations with the people you like most and, to some degree, avoid someone you don't. But if the situation is more dramatic, it might be impossible to suck it up to maintain the group's equilibrium. You might also be able to create a kind of subdivision in your friend group. Remember Michelle Kennedy, who created the mom-friend-finding-app Peanut? She regrets not doing just that:

> I lost a friend at the expense of trying to save a group. We were a group. And this woman, for various, probably silly, micro things, decided she didn't want to be in a group situation anymore. She really didn't want to hang out with the other girls anymore. But she still wanted to maintain a friendship with me. And I was like, "No, come on! It's us four. We're a four. That's who we are!" And ultimately, I lost her completely because of it. I was very hurt. I still am quite hurt about it all these years on. I was hurt, and I extended an olive branch, even though I felt like I'd been wronged.

Unfortunately, the woman wasn't having it. Maybe she felt rejected that Kennedy hadn't stuck with her right away? "I think if I was doing it again, I wouldn't fight for the group. When she came to me and said, 'You know what? I just don't want this anymore. I want to be your friend. Love you. Just don't want to be with the other girls.' I think I should have just said, 'Cool.'"

Another consideration is: What kind of relationship is this? Is this friend someone I've been really close to, or have we just been spending a lot of time together because of circumstance? How much time have you already invested in the friendship?

Maria Menounos told me that some of her friendships weathered her success, and some didn't. "When you're chasing your dream and the success hits, some people are happy for you. Some people are not happy for you. Some people want to grow with you, and some people don't. So, there are unfortunate breakups that occur." Not all changes need to be as unusual as fame, as in Menounos's case. You might want to end a friendship for far less dramatic reasons. You graduate school and change cities for work, and suddenly you're just not thinking about your roommate from the dorm. Your kid goes to a new school, and suddenly those mom-friends fade away. Degges-White told me, "If we think of humans as dynamic, we don't want to stay the same. And if a friendship does not have enough strength and elasticity to allow for change in individuals, the friendship can't change or grow either. And so, friendships will come to an end if they can't allow for that growth." Realizing a friendship isn't going to make it through a transition tells you it was a utility friendship. It's not that it wasn't great; it just wasn't as developed as a core friendship. Or, as Menounos says, "Sometimes you just need to move people to cousin status. I still love them and wish them well, but they get moved to cousin status."

In those situations, you don't need to do much. You can leave more time between calls, make fewer plans—basically do what comes naturally.

Without much practice in how to manage conflict, many women choose to ghost a friend they no longer want in their lives. It's hard to say what is worse, being told that a friend doesn't want to know you anymore or not knowing why a friend has just disappeared. Of course, it's hard to tell someone that your feelings have changed, but you're saving them from spending their emotional energy wondering what has happened.

Anita Chakrabarti says that when women need to talk about friendships in therapy, it's often because a relationship has ended, they don't understand why, and they are often very sad and in a lot of pain: "The idea of Radical Acceptance, as introduced by Tara Brach in her book *Radical Acceptance*, and as further developed by Dr. Marsha Linehan in Dialectical Behavior Therapy, encourages readers to acknowledge what they're feeling in the present moment and allow that experience with acceptance and compassion." Chakrabarti continues,

> Some of the work of psychotherapy is learning how to accept and bear things that previously felt unbearable: facing the reality of a situation with grace and courage rather than looking away and denying that it is happening. When a relationship ends, there can be pain that at times feels physical as well as emotional. But when we learn how to accept the pain, then the suffering recedes, and we start to grow from the experience. Dr. Marsha Linehan identifies a state of mind, "Wise Mind," in which you accept your feelings but also allow yourself to think about what is happening in a more detached and logical way. Wise Mind also contains that little extra something that lets you know that things happen for a reason, and although there is pain in the moment, later when you look back you will realize that you both lost and gained something from

the experience, even if it was painful. Wise mind is that part of your mind that helps you look at things from both sides and helps you learn from all experiences, the good and the bad, to become who you are meant to be.

But sometimes things are more dramatic. Lies. Cheating. Fights. Backstabbing. Manipulation. Those times call for a bigger reaction: the friendship breakup. Sometimes you will be the friend dumper, and sometimes you'll get dumped.

Tracy Moore has been on both sides of this story: "I was a bad friend to someone I met at university. I felt that this woman needed me to be more invested in the relationship, and I didn't want to be. So, instead of actually ending the relationship, I kept being sort of a half-assed friend until the point when she called me on it. It was an awful confrontation." The woman called her at work, making a two-sided heart-to-heart awkward, if not impossible:

> It was very difficult for me to get all vulnerable and into the weeds with a friend who is telling me that I don't care enough and I'm not there enough and I'm not making the time enough. She was right on every single count. She called me, and she was steaming mad. She just told me about myself. And I had no defense. I said, "You're right. I've been a terrible friend." And she said, "Well, it's over." And she dumped me, and I felt really badly about it, but I also completely understood. I wasn't giving her what she was giving me.

When it came time to end a toxic friendship in her life, Moore did not stage a confrontation. She had known this woman since high school. "She was always willing to go out, always game, always up for adventure." Unfortunately, she couldn't tolerate other relationships in Moore's life. Trouble started showing up after Moore went to college. When she'd introduce her old friend to her new college friends, this woman would find a way to drive a wedge into those relationships and break them up. "One by one, every time I introduced her to anyone. I had to bang my head against the walls many times before I got it." So much so that she remained friends with this woman after college for several more years. The woman was a bridesmaid in Moore's wedding to her husband, Lio. But what he revealed to Moore later was the last straw.

Unbeknownst to her, Lio planned a makeover of their home with a well-known TV designer as well as a proposal he would surprise her with at the home reveal. To pull off this dramatic event, he needed her to be out of the city for a few days. He called up the friend and asked if she'd take Moore away for a girls' long weekend. He'd cover the costs of everything—hotel, dinners out, the whole she-bang. "And remember," Moore told me, "this is a friend who is always good to go. And the friend said to Lio, 'Are you sure Tracy wants to marry you?' And he said, 'Well, we've talked about it.' And the friend said, 'Hmmm. I don't know. She really hasn't talked to me about it.' She tried to sabotage my marriage proposal! And I didn't find out until after my wedding. I was like, that's *it*!"

Knowing that this person would never make herself vulnerable enough to have an honest conversation about her behavior over the years led Moore to decide that an explicit "we're done" talk wouldn't be productive. This friend's jealousy had always been evident. She didn't like it when Moore went away to college, and she didn't like it when Moore got her first job in TV. The stunt she pulled with the proposal finally solidified Moore's understanding of this person, and so she just stopped communicating with her. "She was a ticking time bomb. And one of the most fun friends I've ever had in my life."

That's a tricky road to navigate. After you realize someone isn't good to have in your life, you still have to reckon with why they were there in the first place. Moore had so many adventures and so many great times with this person, it's understandable that she found it hard to part with her. "I felt like, 'Can I have these memories but not have you in my life? How does that work? Do I have to throw away everything? All those fun times we went to Miami, the trips to Jamaica—like, do I get rid of them?' And I realized, no, those memories are still good. That was a great time in my life."

Toxic friends wouldn't be in your life if they were that way in every encounter. Particularly if the bad actor has some self-awareness, she'll compensate for her toxic behavior with charm or compliments. Sasha Tong had a friend at college who would seesaw between nastiness and generosity. "She used to walk ahead of me and say really bad things to me. But then she would make me gifts or make me lunch and bring it to my work. It was toxic. And then I found myself using the friendship for the good stuff. Like, I'm a university student, and I have no money, and you're bringing me clothes and stuff." Tong ended the relationship with an email explaining that the friend's behavior was unacceptable. "I remember her writing back and begging me, like, no, no, no. And I remember not writing back and feeling such a freedom after that."

Sometimes you get dumped by a friend but later realize that the feeling was mutual. When Elise Loehnen was dumped by a friend in her early twenties, she never found out why. "In retrospect we had this sort of weird codependency going on where I was almost functioning as her boyfriend. Like, I would fix things; I'd take care of things. And she ditched me with no explanation, and it was so hurtful because I didn't have the closure of knowing what I had done or how I had aggrieved her." Loehnen tried to solicit an explanation from this friend but never received one, even though their social circles overlapped, and they would occasionally see each other. "In retrospect, I'm thrilled because she was consuming."

Sometimes in life you have to do the right thing, and it's really hard. Breaking up with a friend would be one of those times. But the perspective you choose to adopt can radically change your fear or apprehension. Once upon a time, if our marriage didn't last fifty-plus years, we thought of it as a failure. Evolved thinking suggests that's just not the case. And a breakup with one of your friends is much the same. If a friendship ends, and you view it as a failure or a waste of time, you've missed the point and done a great disservice to you both. Start viewing the end as a relationship that has run its course, not one that has been an abject failure. The only failure occurs when you choose to stay in a friendship you consciously know isn't working and can't be fixed. Otherwise, you can still hold on to all of the good times you've shared with another person and look for the lessons and the key takeaways that brought the relationship to an end.

HOMEWORK

Okay, I promised you a map, didn't I? As I've said before, your situation is unique. These are what I believe are reasonable considerations to walk through when you need to end a friendship:

- Make a list. Write down the friendships that feel troubled.

- Can it be fixed? Ask yourself if you have a situation that could be improved, even if it would involve some difficult or uncomfortable conversations? If so, I urge you to give it a shot. The worst thing that can happen is the friendship doesn't survive the process—and you were already considering that! And if you're successful, you've deepened a friendship. But perhaps you've already tried to clear the air, and it hasn't helped. Or maybe you're finally getting some clarity on what has been a longtime pattern.

- Clearly understand your responsibility in the problem. Before you're quick to dismiss this person as toxic or not serving you, look at how you also might have contributed to the problem. Whether you end the friendship or not, it's imperative to your own personal growth as well as the health of your future relationships to understand how you could have been better. Why did you tolerate bad behavior? What in you needed it?

- Imagine your life without this person. It's valuable to picture how that looks and feels. Is it a weight off your shoulders or a gut punch? This is a good exercise for any big decision and can quickly illuminate your true feelings. Consider what else in your life might be changed by the end of this friendship. Are you part of a group? Do your kids love each other? Will you have to let other people know what's going on? Envisioning your new reality can help smooth the often rough transition out of a friendship.

- Does the relationship demand an explicit conversation? It's one thing to allow a workplace friendship to slowly cool without explanation, but if we're talking about someone you've known well for years, you should honor that relationship with a conversation. Or a letter. Or an email. Being direct with a person, even though you might have lost that warm and fuzzy feeling, allows you to still pay respect to the institution of friendship and to the better times you did have with the other person. This is a really difficult thing to do, and upon even thinking about it, a thousand excuses will flood your mind. Take the time to weed out real reasons not to do it versus your own anxiety and fear of talking about it.

- What do you want to communicate? Do you need her to know exactly why you can't continue in the friendship? Does she already know that she's crossed a line with you? Or will it be a shocking piece of news? Try, as best as you can, to be sensitive to her feelings. Even if you plan to speak with her in person, write down your thoughts in advance.

- How do you want to do it? Can you imagine telling her it's over, or are you a better written communicator? If you do it in person, expect it to be emotionally charged! Practice in your head or in the mirror. I'm not joking! It might feel weird, but this is important stuff, and when you actually hear the words out loud, it will affect you. There will be discomfort. So, you want to get as comfortable as you can conveying your message so it doesn't get lost. Letting people know that you don't want to be their friend anymore is about as confrontational as most of us will ever get. If you write her a letter or send an email, be extremely careful with your language. Know for sure that other people are going to read it. Don't swear. Don't smear. Be concise and as gracious as you can muster. That shit is forever.

- Keep your cool. Having come to the conclusion that the friendship is over, it's likely that you have hurt or angry feelings. Try, as best you can, to be sensitive to her feelings in what you say or write. Do not communicate your message as a reaction to something that has happened. No matter what you do, out of respect, you need to have processed your feelings and be clear on your message, and you can't do that if you're reacting in the moment to something. Acting out of a reaction will never bring the desired result. Your anger or hurt will fade, but you'll always feel bad if you're unnecessarily cruel. If the conversation comes as a surprise to her, she might be upset and even cry. She might want to argue about the way you remember things. She might try to change your mind. Imagine various scenarios, and make a plan for how you will respond.

- It hurts, even if you're the one ending it. Give yourself permission to grieve the loss of your friend. There was a reason you were drawn together in the first place, and even though it was ultimately a bad fit, you're entitled to fond memories. And don't even bother feeling guilty for choosing the "wrong" friend. That's life. There really is no such thing. We try on different relationships. Some work, and some don't. Learn and keep it moving.

- Let people know who need to know. If you let people stumble on the information, you're just asking for gossip to swirl around you. Some of your mutual friends might be angry with you, particularly if your ending this friendship creates issues in a shared social circle. Reassure them that they're free to continue their own friendships, but you're also going to make decisions for yourself. You don't have to remain friends with someone to make others more comfortable. Never ask people to take sides. If you feel like you need people to know about something potentially harmful about this person, okay. But other than with your closest ride-or-die, try not to talk shit. And if that's impossible, give yourself a deadline to get it out of your system, and then stop.

- Expect some awkwardness. If you're in a larger social circle, you might run into each other. Maybe you need a break from that group to give your feelings a chance to settle. Create some boundaries for yourself. Are you okay being at a party with her? How about a dinner party? How about a book club? You get to decide what feels comfortable for you. Think about how you'll handle it if you do see each other. What's the briefest, most polite exchange you could have? Role play in your mind the various situations in which you might find yourself with her, and really think about how you'll respond, what energy you'll bring to the situation. My advice is to always take the high road, and if you can't, then you need time away from those situations until you can.

- Make it count. Take the time and energy you were giving to that relationship and put it into the ones that fill you with energy and joy. Take what you've learned through the ordeal and bring it forward into your current or new friendships. This truly is the silver lining of breaking up with someone.

Friendship Scripts

I know these seem like impossible conversations to have. I'm going to give you some scripts. Of course, you'll make these your own, but I hope these will get you started.

> *Your old party pal is still out every night, while you're home with a toddler. She texts three times a week about what an old lady you are, and when are you coming out? When you do get together, the old fun just isn't there. You each have different expectations for your friendship.*

You could say something like:
"I have to say something that is pretty hard. We're in such different places right now. We had so much fun back in the day, and I want to be clear that I'm not judging you for still hitting the town, but I just can't right now. And I don't want to feel bad about it. Honestly, I probably have one night out in me a month, and even then, I want to be in bed by 9:00! I feel like rather than me always saying 'no' to you, it would be better if you had another friend who would say 'yes.' I hope you understand."

> *A newish friend with whom you clicked instantly turns out to support a political agenda you can't abide. Who knew that sometimes they don't wear those hats? You got to know each other in a class, so it took some time for her politics to come up, but by then you were having lunch together twice a week.*

You could say something along the lines of:
"I have to share something with you that is sort of hard for me. We've talked so much about books because of this

course, we really didn't get into our politics until recently. And as we did, I realize that we come from different points of view. It's not that I don't think people of different stripes can't be friends, but I also do try to live my values. And there are things that I find too hurtful and harmful about your political allegiance that I just don't feel right pretending it doesn't matter to me. I hope you'll understand."

She did you dirty. You found out that when she could have said great things about you to a potential employer, she declined. Maybe you'd always wondered if she was jealous of you?

You could try something like:

"I know I've been avoiding you lately, and I wanted to let you know why. I heard about what you said to Pierre. Of course, you're free to say whatever you want or feel. But it made me realize that this relationship isn't what I thought it was. Actually, it reminded me of why I've been uncomfortable with you for a while now. I didn't want to be that person who just ghosts, and so I wanted to let you know it's not working for me—so we don't have to pretend like this is great for both of us."

Two General Scenarios

You have been wronged and, despite trying, can't or don't want to get over it:

"I want to talk to you about something that I have been having a really hard time with. As you know, we had a pretty big falling out when XYZ happened. I am not interested in rehashing things. I know that you apologized sincerely and have been trying to make this friendship work ever since. I want you to know that I heard your apology, appreciate it, and genuinely accepted it. I also want you to know that I, too, have tried to get to a place where we can move forward. Unfortunately, I just can't, or maybe I just won't, but whatever the reason, I don't think it's fair to me to keep trying to spin this in a way that works and to keep feeling guilty or like a failure when it doesn't, or fair to you to keep feeling guilty or like you are spinning your wheels to fix things. It is out of respect for all of the good times we've had together, and the strong feelings I have for you and this relationship, that I feel it is best that we both step away from it. I am not sure if giving us room to breathe will ever bring us back together, but I know not doing so is certain death. I hope you understand and respect my decision."

You just aren't feeling it anymore:

"Thank you for agreeing to talk to me today. I've got to admit this is a pretty difficult conversation to be having. I'd like to start out by saying that I have really loved our relationship in the past, and I feel lucky to have been a part of it. For a time we were as close as two people could be. And I want to thank you for that. Over the past while, however, I have been feeling more and more distance between us. I don't mean physically—we still hang out quite a bit. I mean we just don't feel connected anymore. I'm not sure if you have felt that, too, but I have tried many ways to reinvigorate my feelings, and it still doesn't feel like it is working for me. I know this might sound drastic, but at this point I feel it's better if you and I take a break. I don't want to ghost you or do a slow fadeaway just because that might be easier. I have a lot of respect for our time together, and out of that respect, I owe it to you and this relationship to be as honest as I can be. You have done nothing wrong. I have done nothing wrong. I just feel like our relationship has served its purpose, and I want that to be my memory of it rather than having it degraded by a lack of honesty or a lack of courage. I really hope you can understand and maybe even feel the same way."

What if you get dumped?

1. **Getting ghosted.** Sadly, this is probably the most common way to get dumped by a friend. If you suspect you're being ghosted, take a beat before picking up the phone. How do you feel? Do you miss this person? Is it a relief? If, after considering it, you realize it was not a good relationship for you, then maybe you just let it ride. Or do you know that you've behaved badly in some way and need to at least apologize? If you don't know what's going on and want to know, or you do know and want to clear the air, get in touch. Ask open questions, such as: "Are you okay? Is there anything you want to tell me? Have I done something to upset you?" You can't know if she'll be straight with you, but you'll know you've done everything you can.

2. **Getting dumped face-to-face.** It's hard to hear that someone you've cared for is done with you. Don't feel like you need to respond to anything in the moment. In fact, it's probably best if you don't. If your friend is angry or upset with you, you need a minute to really think about what she's saying rather than defend yourself or beg for forgiveness. Is what she said true? Did you take her for granted, steal her man, skip her wedding, gossip about her, or whatever it is? Can you make a fulsome apology for your actions? It might not repair what's been broken, but you'll

both feel better if you acknowledge the truth of her claim. And what if it's not true? You really didn't lie, cheat, forget her birthday, or what have you. Again, take a moment to think about your friendship. Was it really working for you? Maybe you hadn't noticed its decline? Is your ego just bruised, or is this really a loss for you? This could be an opportunity to let go of a friendship that's run its course. If you didn't see this coming at all (not the way it was done, but that it was even an option), you need to have a long hard look at your own self. How could you not be dialed in, even a little, that the other person was so unhappy or unfulfilled in this relationship? All of the information counts in these types of situations, so if you hadn't been paying attention up until now, it's time to do so.

3. **Either way, it sucks.** Allow yourself the grace to be sad. Or mad. Or both. Eventually, you'll likely see how this friendship fits into your story, and you'll learn more about yourself. Do you need more boundaries? Do you need to be more available? Do you need to share more? Are you perfect, and she was an idiot? Give yourself time for it all to make sense.

I met my friend Sanna, when I was twenty-one or twenty-two, at a party in the East Village. She is Swedish, and I am from Norway.

We had an instant connection, and when we first met, in a very weird, fundamental sense, I don't know what it was, but she was everything that I was not, and vice versa. We just complemented each other.

We had known each other for maybe four years, five years before 9/11.

I had moved back to Norway at the time, but I was still going back and forth to New York a lot. I came to New York to do a photo shoot with a photographer from Norway and decided to stay with Sanna in Brooklyn while he stayed uptown around Times Square.

She is a real hustler. She was about seven months pregnant, supporting her husband, cooking with one hand, making work calls with the other hand. She's a very full-on person. The morning of 9/11, I woke up early to make a meeting down on Canal Street. Sanna was already up and out of the house before me. I decided to take a car to my meeting, and suddenly it had to turn around at the Brooklyn Bridge—but nobody knew why.

So I took the subway, but it kept stopping. The energy started to get kind of claustrophobic and scary. And then someone comes running into the car and starts talking, in a panicked tone, about something that was going on. I was trying to overhear what they were saying, I couldn't make it out, but something was obviously very wrong. Finally, a couple of minutes later, the subway just stops permanently, a couple of blocks from Canal Street, which is pretty close to the Twin Towers. I exited the station and I looked up and I couldn't connect the dots. Something overtook me. Everybody was just . . . in a state. I can't describe it. The only thing I could think of, the only thing I could understand was: *I need to find my friend.* Not I need to call my parents and let them know I'm okay. Not I need to find the Norwegian photographer who doesn't know his way around New York. I just need to find my friend."

Of course, nobody's cell phone works. And for every pay phone, there were at least twenty people waiting. And then the dust starts rolling in. And all I can hear is helicopters roaring like I'm in the middle of a war zone.

I finally got to the front of a pay-phone line, but I couldn't get through. Every line just rang busy. I knew I had to make my way to Times Square to get to the hotel so I could call her.

So on I walked all the way to Times Square in my high heels. The hotel wouldn't let me in because I wasn't a guest, but I found a pay phone. I tried to call, but it wouldn't go through, so I finally called my mother in Norway and got ahold of her. I said, 'Here's Sanna's number. Please call her.

Keep trying her until you can get her, give her this address, ask her to come down here.' After that, I just slumped down in front of the hotel and waited. And waited. At about 10 p.m. that night, Sanna showed up at the front of the hotel. She had walked down from wherever she was. I can't describe my feeling seeing her. We hugged and cried. She hadn't been able to get ahold of her boyfriend (the father of her child) or any family members. We decided to walk to Chelsea to her boyfriend's mother's place to create a home base.

Though we don't speak all the time and have only seen each other a handful of times since then, whenever something really challenging has come up in my life—a sick child, a divorce—we always reach out to one another, almost instinctually. And every time something like that happens and I reconnect with her, a sense of joy washes over me. *I'm so happy I found Sanna. And she found me.*"

TONJE KRISTIANSEN
on friends in a storm

CHAPTER 10

How to Make
New Friends

*You can't stay in your corner of the Forest waiting for
others to come to you. You have to go to them sometimes.*

A. A. MILNE, *Winnie-the-Pooh*

ioneering astronomer Maria Mitchell wrote about
friendship in her diary in 1855,

> [I am] resolved to have more balanced relationships.
> . . . How unwise it is to turn a single person into
> the center of gravity in one's emotional universe.
> Instead, one's attachments should be distributed
> among many people, each fulfilling a different
> need—one providing intellectual stimulation, another
> rendering us more elastic and buoyant, happier and
> radiating more happiness, because we know him,
> another inspiring in us such warmth and affection
> that our hearts grow as if in a summer feeling.

This idea spoke to me in a couple of ways. In a friendship that's right, there should be an easiness in the beginning of the union, and yet, at the same time, some amount of strategy—actively filling in your friend circle in an effort to expand yourself. We discussed in chapter 8 the importance of understanding the different roles of the friends in your life, and in doing so, you might have realized you've got some holes to fill. The passage from Mitchell's diary also underscores the importance of making new friends. As we evolve, so does what we need from our friendships. Life drops us in different places in time, and if we are to grow, we are obligated to find people who will fulfil different needs.

Some relationships last a lifetime and can evolve as you do. Some, however, only make sense in a specific framework. You bond with someone while taking a course together, but your friendship doesn't really hold up outside of that setting. You were tight with someone who was a blast to party with, but after you outgrew going out until 2 a.m. four nights a week, the friendship didn't make the transition. And that's okay. But it might mean there are times when you need to find new friends that better reflect where you are in life. You just had kids and crave time with other new moms. You started a business and want to hang out with other entrepreneurs. You've moved to a new city. You've got a new job. You've embraced your health in a big way. Being self-aware about where you are in life and what you need in your friendships will help you mindfully choose new relationships.

At the beginning of the book, we discussed the importance of close friends to your overall health and mental well-being. The science is in. Even their absence has been studied. Dutch sociologist Gerald Mollenhorst showed that both after marrying and after having kids, people let go of a significant percentage of their close friends. Furthermore, and this is a little scarier, German researchers conducting a meta-analysis concluded that globally, friendship networks have been shrinking for the past thirty-five years: Between 1980 and 1985, participants reportedly had four more friends on average, compared with the participants who'd taken part in studies between 2000 and 2005. Knowing what we know about the personal health benefits and the community health benefits of friendships combined with the alarming rate of burnout, now more than ever we need to start turning this friend reduction trend around.

As I looked at the numbers of friends dropping both after marriage and after kids, I was reminded of a phenomenon famed couples psychotherapist and podcast host Esther Perel often speaks about: "Today, we turn to one person, our partner, to provide what an entire village once did: a sense of grounding, meaning, and continuity." A decrease in these networks not only has the potential to do us harm, physiologically and emotionally, but also poses a real threat by increasing pressure within our romantic relationships. If you expect your partner to be all things to you, you're going to be disappointed. "Today," Perel goes on to say, "I am meditating on the importance of the village: how I have built my village and how you can build and maintain yours. Remember: it is the quality of our relationships that determines the quality of our lives." For many of us, that means it's time to do the hard work of cultivating greatness in both old and new friends.

The problem with all of this is that, if you're anything like me, the idea of starting a new friendship seems overwhelming. In fact, more than a handful of the women I interviewed for this book had at least a subtle *no new friends* vibe, and trust me, I could relate. As I examined my own great hesitation, I realized that much of it was fear-based. The very idea of putting myself out there and having to reveal the good, the bad, the ugly of me made me wonder if mediocrity was really that bad. Surely, all of the friends I had in my roster were *good enough*. And yet, when I consider my recent foray into the new-mom world (a world I was initially adamant about staying out of), I realize I have forged some of my most memorable friendships yet. These new friends have unlocked in me things that (1) I didn't know existed, and (2) I really love about myself.

But how do you do it? First things first, you have to know where the friendship gaps are in your life. Back in chapter 7 you did a diagnosis of your friendships. You took a look at what kinds of friends you have and where you're maybe feeling a lack. Remember, it's not about getting everything from each friend—it's perfectly normal to have friends with different roles in your life. Times of change in your life are good moments to consider your roster, but even if you haven't made a big shift, it's worth considering every once in a while.

The other element to consider is your capacity. Are you frantically running from work to home to extended family? Then maybe you just want to shore up your current friendships and make sure you get time with those friends. But maybe there are times when you could use a little more human contact (and less binging reality TV). Think about what you have to give in terms of time and energy.

My new friend Emilie moved to the United States from France more than six years ago for her work as an advertising executive. At first, she thought it was a short-term move, so she put all her friendship energy into maintaining relationships back home. "I felt really heartbroken to leave my friends, but I always thought I'd come back, so I really didn't work on friendships because in my mind I would never stay here." She spent a lot of time calling and texting her friends in France, worried that the distance might pull them apart. And then she met her husband, Spencer. "Then Spencer was my best friend. At the same time, I was thinking, 'I have friends, I have friends!' but I really wasn't investing too much. And I think it's now that I'm coming to the point that I actually need to make friends because I'm coming to the realization that my life is here."

As well as realizing she has to make time and space for friends in her new city of Los Angeles, Emilie also had to grapple with complicated feelings about replacing her old friends. "I don't want to let go of my friends. I'm not dedicating as much time to them as I'd like. I'm afraid these friendships are going to disappear." But friendships don't function like clothing swaps. Your new friends don't need to fit exactly in the holes left by other friends. And if you're experiencing guilt over your new friendships, you might be bringing that energy along with you.

My friend Helene Corneau-Cohen's life has forced her to learn the art of friend-making over and over again. When her kids were small, she, like many parents, gravitated to friendships that incorporated the parents of her children's friends. "Obviously, you make lots of acquaintances through your kids. And if you're lucky, you'll make a select few amazing, beautiful, and lasting friendships. And thanks to our girls, I did!"

As her kids grew up and left home, she found herself in a new chapter of relationships. "I became an empty nester, and making friends seemed like a whole new ballgame as you no longer have the opening ticket of a child or two!" This was also a time when she and her husband were moving frequently. "I often found myself in new and foreign environments where I did not know a single soul. I had to find a few lovely friends to share moments with. At that point, meeting someone you want to invite into your world rests on your choice alone. It becomes much more about chemistry and personal affinities." No longer having the day-to-day responsibilities of parenthood allowed her more time for friendships. She observed that life experience gave her a clearer idea of the kinds of friends she'd want to make time for. "I would say that it is challenging and time consuming, and you must be willing to put in the time and effort into a new friendship; otherwise it's pointless. Now more than ever before, I'm being really intentional about who my friends are. It's really about who do I like, who do I gel with; it's less about the more functional need of my old mom friends."

When it comes to the question of how to make a new friend, Helene says, "Every occasion could potentially be a favorable situation to meet new friends. A yoga class, the park, a talk, or a dinner party could all be ground for a new beginning, as long as you are open to it and feel a connection at some level."

This book was written at a time when making new friends was extra challenging, thanks to COVID-19. So many of us were homebound and unable to do more than have Zoom cocktails with our existing friends, let alone find new ones. As I've said before, however, it did provide some of us lots of time to consider what we want going forward. Entrepreneur and lifestyle influencer Chriselle Lim realized during quarantine that her workaholic style might need a shakeup. "I've always been the one to find the most ridiculous excuses not to go out. I'll throw my kids under the bus, like, 'Oh, she's sick, I can't make it!' I've realized during this time that I can't be like that all the time." Time stuck at home has made her realize the value friendships could bring to her life. "So, coming out of this, I think I should and will be more open to relationship building—outside of my immediate family and my one best friend."

Making new friends can certainly feel challenging or like more effort than it's worth, but after reading all of the research, I believe the benefits far outweigh the discomfort. But how do you do it, exactly? In studying this, I stumbled across a great piece on Psyche.com by psychologist Marisa Franco. She boils down the process to four relatively easy steps.

Assume that people like you: "Forms of avoidance are caused by understandable fears of rejection . . . If you go into social situations with a positive mind-set, assuming people like you, then it's more likely that this will actually turn out to be the case."

Initiate: "To embrace the importance of initiating, you must let go of the myth that friendship happens organically. You have to take responsibility rather than waiting passively. But it's not just showing up that matters, it's saying 'hello' when you get there."

Keep showing up: "If you want to make friends, you should commit to showing up somewhere for a few months. If you go to one event, feel uncomfortable, and don't return, you're selling yourself short. If you persist, you'll feel more comfortable, get to know people more, and—thanks in part to the mere exposure effect (our tendency to like things more the more familiar they seem)— they'll come to like you more as time goes on."

Get vulnerable: "I like to think of an acquaintance as someone you know of, whereas a friend is someone you know. To make true friends, you have to share things about yourself and ask people questions so that they share about themselves too. You don't have to share whatever you might tell a therapist, but, deepest darkest secrets aside, you still have much to share."

The attitude summed up by these rules is a positive one. Trust yourself! Take a shot! Take a few shots! It's all going to be fine. Approach friend-making like the fun adventure it is. So, after you're clear on where the holes are in your life, you can begin, strategically, to fill them.

How to Make a Nostalgic Friend

You can't go backward, so there's no creating a friendship that started when you were eight and continued until today. But if you're craving a connection to a certain time in your life, that's something you can make happen. Social media makes it relatively easy to find people from our past. Get clear about what it is you're looking for. Was there a classmate that just got your bizarro sense of humor? Was there a person on your track and field team who brought out your inner competitor? Was there someone in an early job who fired you up intellectually? Is there something about *you* that this person knows that you'd like to keep alive? Was there a time when you were crazier, more determined, more creative? Could having someone in your life that you shared that time with bring that back to the fore?

Remember the fondness I have for my time growing up at the lake? About six months ago, when things were really starting to get crazy in the United States, I was feeling a growing sense of anxiety that couldn't be squashed. By sheer good luck (or maybe it was the universe answering my call), as I was doing my daily scrolls through Instagram, I got a friend request from an old Winnipeg friend, Levy. My heart immediately filled with joy, and I accepted. I spent the next fifteen minutes devouring all the pictures on Levy's feed, most of which were from good old Deception Bay, Lake of the Woods. I was overjoyed. I could have left it there or continued to silently stalk. But my response was so visceral that I knew I had a hole to fill. Maybe it was just the country I missed, maybe it was the Canadian people I missed, or maybe it was specifically Levy-baby, but either way I knew I needed to connect. I reached out, directly, and we've been chatting ever since. I hadn't known I needed it, and I could have easily missed the invitation to engage if I hadn't had this new mindset on friendship and being intentional about what really matters to me.

How to Make a Nurturing Friend

If you'd like the empty seat on your friend-team's bench to go to a nurturer, you'll have to find your own soft side first. Caring and vulnerability won't likely make themselves apparent in a relationship that's all about wry observations and sarcastic jokes (not that there's anything wrong with either of those things). We sometimes think thoughtful and nurturing friends can come only from our past. And that can be true—if you've known them for years, their affection for you runs deep. But this kind of person can arrive on the scene at any time. In fact, the worst of times can bring out people's true colors in unexpected ways.

Remember Lindzi Scharf from chapter 1? Her daughter's diagnosis with a serious medical condition rendered her more in need of friends than ever. "You hear people say, 'Yeah, but would they take you to the airport?' like somehow that's the barometer of a friendship. To me, it became, 'Yeah, but would they show up at the hospital for you?'" She was surprised to see who that would be. "My younger brother has really risen to the occasion. He stepped up in a way that I never could have imagined. I don't just think of him as my brother. He's my friend."

How to Make a Creative Friend

The great thing about creative people is that they can be found just about everywhere. And their energy and general sparkiness make them easy to spot.

Workplaces are probably the most common location to make a creative friend. When you feel that extra spark with a workmate, it's not hard to lean in to that feeling. Ask her out for lunch or to take a walking break with you. Look for ways to collaborate more at work. Be sure to throw shine on her ideas in meetings, and ask for her input on your work.

You might cross paths with a new creative friend in random places—at a dinner party, at the dog park, at day-care pickup. And maybe the trickiest part is that you have to be willing to take the leap when you meet a friend that you spark with. I was recently on Maria Menounos' show *Better Together,* and we really hit it off. But you never know when you're doing media interviews. I mean, it's a host's job to be friendly! But she told me later, "In the last couple of years, I've really worked hard on when I meet someone like you and we connect and I'm like, wow, we're like-minded, she's smart, she's on the same path as me—I'm going to really make the time to get to know this person. And I've been doing that. And I was like, 'I want to be friends!'" And sure enough, within days we had a two-hour, nonstop-talking brunch.

Menounos continues, "It is a little bit more awkward as you get older to make new friends, but I know that your peer group is important to your growth. I've really been cultivating some really great friendships with people I respect, and it's cool. You grow, learn together, and you have fun together."

How to Make a Mentor Friend

This is one of the easiest friendships to cultivate. In a mentor, you're not looking for someone to spend an enormous amount of time with. And the time you spend together tends to be quite focused. You're discussing a new project, you're going over options, you're testing out some new ideas. Start by thinking of where in your life you could use a mentor. Do you need some wisdom when it comes to marriage? Work? Parenting? All of the above?

Next, find your mentor. Perhaps there's already someone in your life you look up to, and you could focus your energy on that person. If there isn't, don't despair. Look further afield. Who is ten years ahead of you (in whatever capacity) and seems inspiring? Do your homework (even though you'll feel creepy).

If your kid is just starting kindergarten, scope out the playground for the moms of older kids who seem like they're managing things in a way that looks good to you. That might mean they're obviously working full time, or it might mean they're fully committed to parent council. This isn't about judgment; it's about cultivating a relationship that will guide you.

If you're hoping for a mentor of a more professional nature, be sure to know as much as you can about her work. Read her articles, watch her TED Talk on YouTube, follow her on LinkedIn. When you reach out, don't go cap in hand. Offer something up. Your email might come with an article attached that you think could be of interest to her. Be sure to acknowledge the most recent piece of work of hers you've seen or heard about. Don't be too thirsty—you don't need to ask if she'll be your mentor. Ask if she'll meet for a quick coffee to talk about *something specific*. If you have some chemistry, make another coffee date. And so on. The trick with any mentor friendship is not to allow it to become one way. Be conscious of offering value in return, and ask if there's any way for you to be of service to her.

My friend Anne had someone in her life for years before that person became her mentor:

> Christina was my boss years ago. To be honest, I
> never really felt like I had her support, and it was
> tough. But somehow once we weren't working together
> anymore, something shifted. She did a lot of personal
> and professional work on herself, and we actually
> had a pretty candid conversation about what kind of
> boss she'd been to me. And I think I'd also become
> confident enough to ask for her help. Now we go out
> for lunch about twice a year, and I absolutely go to
> those lunches with questions and ideas that I want her
> feedback on. And she'll tell me what she thinks. I was

once going for an interview, and I was telling her, "I'm going to just see how it goes," and she said, "No. That is the wrong approach. Go in there and blow them away. You can always turn it down, but you need to blow it out of the water." And she reminded me of all the skills and experience I had that made me right for that gig. She was completely right. In our earlier relationship I would have felt defensive, but now I just really look forward to being coached by her.

How to Make a Vital Friend

If the position of vital friend remains vacant in your life, you should probably start by looking at your existing friends. Is there a reason your good friends aren't best friends? Could you invest the time and energy into upgrading one or two friendships to reach the pinnacle? Or is there some reason you've been holding back? If you want to make a new friend into a vital friend, you're going to have to be patient. Remember what we learned from Robin Dunbar? It takes 200 hours to become close friends—and that's if we use those 200 hours to truly connect, not just be in each other's presence.

But you absolutely can have the friend version of love at first sight. And if the friendship starts off with a lot of energy, you can announce those feelings. Again, from Menounos: "That's what Gabby Bernstein did to me on my podcast." Menounos was interviewing the author and motivational speaker, and it was going really well. "And she was like, 'I love you, and we are going to be best friends!' And I said, 'Oh, my god, I love you!'"

Of course, you still have to put in the time and see if that first spark plays out as a sustainable connection, but it's an exciting way to start!

How to Make a Friend Like You

This kind of friend might mirror you in many ways. If you're an artsy vegetarian who volunteers at an animal shelter, it's unlikely that you're going to hit it off with a steak-loving banker. Just doing the things you love will put you in the company of others with your interest and values. But you have to get out and do some things if you want to meet new people. It's easy to get stuck in a schedule rut. We go to work, we come home, we flake in front of a screen. You have to break that cycle to bring new friends into your life. Sign up for a class. Volunteer. Say yes to party invitations.

Other times you need a new friend to mirror you in a particular way because of a new situation or life stage. It's exactly why Michelle Kennedy—remember her from chapter 4?—created Peanut, the friend-finding app for mothers. Having a baby makes it instantly essential that you know other mothers. The learning curve is so steep that you need the support of other women also going through it. It also means that those friendships develop very quickly.

You can use apps such as Peanut, Bumble BFF, Hey! VINA, Nextdoor, and others to find new friends according to your interests and location. But if that's not your thing, you have to get yourself into circles that support your life stage or situation. You could join a place of worship, take a class, or join a professional association.

And after you're out there, keep your eyes and ears open to interesting new people. Be friendly. Give compliments. Everyone likes to feel liked, so if you give off those vibes, you improve your odds at making a new friend.

How to Meet a Friend Not Like You

This is trickier, obviously. And it can feel a little calculated and even fetishizing. I am definitely not saying that you should go out and find a token friend who will make you look cool or progressive. What I really mean here is being open to stepping outside of your echo chamber. You don't have to hang out with people whose values you find objectionable, but rather you can expand your circle to include people with experiences different from your own. Do you know someone who was raised in another country? Do you know someone who has decided she doesn't want kids? Do you know someone who skipped college and traveled the world instead? You get the idea.

These kinds of connections can often be made through adjacent friends. Maybe my friend Sunny Hasselbring has a stay-at-home-mom friend she's always talking about, and I could ask them both out for coffee. Her choices are different from mine, but getting to know someone like her better could teach me a lot. Again, putting yourself in new situations by volunteering or signing up for a class is also a way to meet people you might not normally connect with.

HOMEWORK

- Take note of the friendship holes you
  have from the chapter 7 homework.

- Create a game plan for how you might
  connect with this type of person. Write down
  where and when you might be most likely
  to meet this person. Schedule something.

- Let people know that you're on the
  market! You never know who's got
  a friend that could be perfect.

- Get out there! You're not going to
  meet anyone watching Netflix.

CONCLUSION

After spending the past eight months researching and writing about friendship, I want nothing more than to live alone on a desert island for the foreseeable future. *Kidding*! But I was surprised by how many times I felt exhausted. I have discovered so many things that I either took for granted or simply wasn't aware of. Like anything in your life, when you stop to take an inventory, there is often much that has gone unseen or untended to, but there is something particularly complex about looking at friendships because of their relational quality. When you stop to take stock of your health—the food you are eating or the exercise you are doing, it is linear and one directional. When you stop to look at your education or your career history, it is linear—you have a relationship with your work or your studies. All of these cases are examples of you versus the inanimate, how you have or have not found your groove orbiting around something. When you start to unfold your present and past behavior and experience in friendship, however, there are not just two active things at play but an infinite number of things at play, when you factor in different personalities, different understandings, and different situations for each relationship. Add to that not having the clear benchmarks or expectations other types of relationships do. It all adds up to a lot of grey in how to really do friendship right. But I can truly say that coming out on the end of all of the work has left me feeling light, free, and renewed in a way that I haven't in a long, long time. The beauty and power in true friendship simply can't be duplicated in any other way.

One of the things that surprised me the most was how much work is required by the individual to create successful friendships. It's counterintuitive that it's not mostly about *two* people. In other words, so much of the upfront work is personal—understanding who you are, what you truly want and need, and how you're going to get it—it all seemed so very me, me, me! But when you think about it, if both parties are doing their own work on themselves, really putting honesty and communication forward, then there can be perfect balance. The relationship can be what it needs to be for both and operate on its highest plane. When you do the work on yourself and expect the other to do the same, the relationship is left to thrive rather than carry the burden of ambivalence or resentment.

I guess I shouldn't have been surprised that my first lesson on awakening to my own friendships came with the very announcement of this book to said friends. They all had different reactions—so telling. Friends I never thought would take an interest pleasantly surprised me by wanting to weigh in; friends I thought would be far more invested really disappointed me; some friends did exactly what I had expected they would, and this gave me great comfort. In the many conversations I have had with friends, on the record, for the book, I have been shown the error of my ways at least a handful of times: learning about Jette Miller's past trauma and how my behavior had been triggering, hearing I had dropped the ball once in an exchange with Michal Steel, being too distant in times of conflict with Sophie . . . the list goes on. It was humbling, to say the least, especially for someone who thought she was doing so well!

But it was also empowering. When people are honest and open, and you create a forum for it, you really feel like the strength of the relationship has your back, and it's pretty amazing. All of these conversations were not only growth moments for the relationships but also most definitely for me as an individual. I have to say it has been interesting and cathartic to shift my energy based on people's actions, as opposed to our shared history or habit, and see how the relationship shifts. It has almost had a Ouija board quality to it, like now that I've started to really pay attention and give or take energy away, the relationship, much like the little plastic handset, starts to feel like it's shifting on its own. This has just served to add to that magic feeling friendship can ignite.

As we face the world today, much is uncertain. There has been a growing trend of disconnection or fragmentation through the increased use of social media. We have much busier lives, in which meaningful connection has been bumped off the schedule until next week, *again*. And now, quite literally, we have been physically isolated in quarantine for more than a year, at the hands of a global pandemic. When I sold the idea for this book, we needed to work on our friendships, and as I handed in my first completed draft, as I saw it, we didn't have a choice. We can either begin to make meaning and make choices toward empathy, connection, and wholeness, or we can continue to bury our heads in our devices until we run out of batteries, for good. If anything, the silver lining of this grueling time in quarantine is that it has served to put us on notice. We have physically been pulled away from those we love, but will we make it count or just go back to business as usual?

This means getting comfortable with the short-term uncomfortable. So difficult for a culture obsessed with ease and convenience! That means working on vulnerability to build up our strength. Also difficult because most of our role models these days, politically and in the media, prize a strength-at-any-cost attitude. This means being kind. Kind to ourselves and to others. If ripping off the Band-Aid and doing full analysis feels like too much right at this moment, then I encourage you to be kind to yourself by honoring where you are, and just start by doing something kind and unexpected for a friend. Send a postcard out of the blue saying something nice. Write a letter recalling a sentimental moment shared. Write a journal entry about a moment in friendship you wouldn't give up for anything. Find a way to tell someone you love them. Do what you need to do to get the conversation started, both with yourself and with the other.

If you have made it to the end of this book, I thank you for your time and attention, and the type A in me is full of love and appreciation for the student in you. But now, it is time to throw off your cap and get out of your head and into the world to make choices, changes, and commitments to the only people who have the power to make an intolerable life tolerable, a mediocre life good, and a good life great: your friends.

ACKNOWLEDGMENTS

This book, literally, could not have been written without the experience, lessons, and love I've had with my girlfriends—you know who you are!

To my family, who supports and puts up with me, no matter what . . . and whom I also consider my best friends.

To all of the incredible women who shared their insight and their personal stories with me for the book, a HUGE thank you.

To Leila Campoli, my agent at Stonesong—who went above and beyond in the process to help make this book the best it could be—your attention to detail and hard work is so very appreciated.

To my editor, Diana Ventimiglia, who has championed my work not once, but twice—either a genius or a fool—thank you so much!

And last but not least, to Jocelyn, who continues to set the bar for what true friendship ought to be, you are gone but never forgotten.

ABOUT THE AUTHOR

Erin Falconer is an author, digital entrepreneur and Psychotherapist. In 2018, she released the critically acclaimed self-improvement/female empowerment book, *How To Get Shit Done: Why Women Need To Stop Doing Everything So They Can Achieve Anything.* Since 2008, she has been the editor-in-chief and co-owner of PickTheBrain. PickTheBrain is not only a great passion project but is also one of the most trusted self-improvement websites and communities on the web. With over 400 bloggers from around the world contributing content, named to over 100 "best of the web" lists, and read in more than 35 countries daily, under Erin's guidance, PTB has truly become a powerful global voice and brand in the self-improvement space. In 2017, off of her blog, Erin launched the PickTheBrain Podcast which ranks consistently in the top 20 in the heath and self-improvement categories on iTunes and in 2018 was featured on the iTunes homepage, twice.

Erin has been heralded as one of the most influential female voices online. PickTheBrain has been named a top motivation blog for 2017 by WealthyGorilla. She was designated one of the top digital entrepreneurs in Los Angeles by *LA Confidential Magazine* as well as being honored by Cadillac & Refinery29 as one of the "Top 7 Women Changing the Digital Landscape for Good." In 2013 *Forbes Magazine* named Falconer's blog one of the "Top 100 Most Influential Sites for Women" (alongside such powerhouses as Pinterest, BlogHer, and Hello Giggles, among others). In 2014, *The Wall Street Journal* included

Erin in their prestigious "Women of Note" network, an exclusive network of powerful female leaders, designed to recognize and foster the continued success of innovative women. In 2019, Maria Shriver noted Erin as one of the year's Architects of Change.

Erin is also the co-founder of LEAFtv, a video lifestyle brand for the millennial woman. In 2015, LEAFtv was sold to publicly traded Demand Media—now trading as The Leaf Group. As a result of her work with LEAFtv she was honored as one of the Top 10 Most Influential Women in Tech. Erin is a very well-respected voice in the self-improvement space, she has produced over 1000 viral videos and has over 900,000 followers on social media.

She lives in Venice with her husband and young son, George.

ABOUT SOUNDS TRUE

Sounds True is a multimedia publisher whose mission is to inspire and support personal transformation and spiritual awakening. Founded in 1985 and located in Boulder, Colorado, we work with many of the leading spiritual teachers, thinkers, healers, and visionary artists of our time. We strive with every title to preserve the essential "living wisdom" of the author or artist. It is our goal to create products that not only provide information to a reader or listener but also embody the quality of a wisdom transmission.

For those seeking genuine transformation, Sounds True is your trusted partner. At SoundsTrue.com you will find a wealth of free resources to support your journey, including exclusive weekly audio interviews, free downloads, interactive learning tools, and other special savings on all our titles.

To learn more, please visit SoundsTrue.com/freegifts or call us toll free at 800.333.9185.